QUILTS *for all* SEASONS
Year-Round Log Cabin Designs

Christal Carter

That Patchwork Place®

Credits

Editor . . . . Ursula Reikes
Copy Editor . . . . Liz McGehee
Text and Cover Design . . . . Kay Green
Photography . . . . Brent Kane
Illustration and Graphics . . . . . . Laurel Strand
                               Stephanie Benson

Acknowledgments

Sincere thanks go to the group of talented quilters who helped with the realization of my designs and whose work appears in this book. Those women include Sandy Andersen, Patty Barney, Carol Hayes, Elizabeth Haynes, Laurine Leeke, Carole O'Brien, Linda Packer, and my special friend, Shirley Baker. A very special thank-you goes to Sharyn Craig, who took time out from a busy schedule to gather this group, prepare brunches, make phone calls, and give me peace of mind. I offer a warm collective hug to you all.

I would also like to thank my dear friends, Carole Nicolay and Donna Sowers, for their help and encouragement, my daughter Catrina for her design suggestions, and my husband, Bill, for all the computer lessons and general guidance.

Dedication

This body of work is dedicated to Bill, who has been the number one encourager and helpmate in my quilting career, and also my best friend through twenty-seven years of marriage.

Quilts for all Seasons: Year-Round Log Cabin Designs ©
© 1993 by Christal Carter

That Patchwork Place, Inc.
PO Box 118
Bothell, WA 98041-0118
USA

Printed in the United States of America
97 96 95 94 93   6 5 4 3 2

Library of Congress Cataloging-in-Publication Data

Carter, Christal.
    Quilts for all Seasons :year-round Log Cabin designs / Christal Carter.
       p. cm.
    ISBN 1-56477-022-2 :
    1. Patchwork—Patterns. 2. Quilting—Patterns.
    I. Title.
TT835.C38 1993   92-39068
746.46—dc20   CIP

Contents

INTRODUCTION

I cannot remember a time when my life has not been deeply affected by the changing seasons. From wonderful childhood memories in Kansas and Southern California to my quilting travels coast to coast and beyond, I have in my mind's eye a lovely, seasonal memory collage. Today as I write, I can smell the sweet spring orange blossoms that perfume the valley where I live. But no less special are the memories of eating sun-warmed apricots and picking cherries and roses in summer, crunching brilliant maple leaves on a brick walkway in autumn, or watching my young daughters make sparkling snow angels at the cabin on a cold winter day. Each season has its own charm, its own wonderful surprises and excitement.

And each time the next season opens up to me, I feel the need to change the surroundings of my home: to change colors, floral arrangements, and of course, quilts. This book was designed with those special changes in mind and with the hope that you will cherish the joys and changes of season that life brings.

GENERAL GUIDELINES

Materials and Equipment

Rotary Cutter and Mat

The indispensible rotary cutter not only saves time for quilters but also improves accuracy. It is a real must for the patterns in this book. I prefer to use the cutter with the larger blade. If you cannot find one in a store near you, they are readily available through mail order.

The rotary cutter cannot be used without a mat. These mats are specially made for rotary cutters and will last for years. I have been using the same mat for thirteen years, and it seems to be none the worse for wear. Mats with the premarked grids are helpful in keeping the fabric straight.

Sharp Fabric-Cutting Scissors

A pair of good scissors is a wonderful investment for any type of sewing. You may also want to purchase a whetstone to sharpen your scissors. A good shop will sell whetstones along with the scissors and should take the time to show you how to use them. I sharpen my own scissors, saving both time and money.

Paper-Cutting Scissors

These could be a pair of old or inexpensive scissors to use for cutting freezer paper and patterns. Cutting paper will quickly dull a good pair of scissors.

Embroidery Scissors

A pair of small, sharp scissors is helpful in cutting small pieces of fabric for appliqué and embroidery work and also for snipping quilting threads during hand quilting.

Sewing Machine

All of the projects in this book can be pieced by machine. A good-quality machine is invaluable. Before beginning any machine work, make sure the machine is clean and oiled. Replace the needle following every eight hours of sewing. Use a needle for "fine" fabrics with these small Log Cabin blocks.

Marking Tools

Water-soluble fabric marking pens
Number 2 lead pencils
White dressmaker's pencil for marking dark fabrics
Colored pencils to color quilt plans and blocks

Rulers

You will need a clear acrylic quilter's ruler to cut strips. These come in a variety of widths and lengths. I prefer a width of 3″ and a length of 24″, with lines marked every ¼″ to ½″. Most of the strips you will cut for these projects require 1″-wide strips.

It is also helpful to have a square plastic ruler, such as the 6″ Bias Square®, for squaring your blocks.

Other Equipment

Light Box. This wooden box, fitted with a clear glass or acrylic top and a light underneath, is used for tracing purposes. Make your own by putting a small lamp under a glass-topped coffee table. Some of my students use their dining table, separated in the middle where the leaves would go. Cover the gap with a piece of heavy glass and put a lamp under the table. It is a good height for tracing.

Iron and Ironing Board

Hoops. Both embroidery and quilting hoops are needed for these projects.

Quilting Frame. This is optional but is helpful in hand quilting or while basting or pinning quilt tops in preparation for hand or machine quilting.

Needles. You will need the following for the projects in this book:

> Small sharps for appliqué
> Quilting needles for hand quilting
> Machine needles
> Embroidery needles for embroidery

Thimbles

Interfacing. Have both fusible and nonfusible interfacing on hand.

Thread. You will need the following types of thread:

> Machine sewing thread
> Embroidery floss
> Quilting thread

Tracing paper

Clear template plastic or cardboard for making templates

Black permanent felt-tip pen, fine point

Roll of freezer paper for appliqué (available in grocery stores)

Miscellaneous notions for these patterns include such items as bias tape, buttons, rickrack, quilt batting, and cording.

Fabrics

Fabric Content

As a general rule, 100% cotton fabrics are the best choices for the patterns in this book. The fabrics should be similar in weight and texture and also colorfast.

For hand appliqué work and for blind-stitch machine appliqué, 100% cotton is preferable. It is easy to work with when folding under the raw edges. If you are not sure of a particular fabric's content but would like to use it for appliqué, try the following quick test. Tightly pinch a folded edge of the fabric and see if a crease line remains. If a line is plainly visible, the fabric will probably work well for appliqué. If no crease forms and the fabric is difficult to "finger press," it is more likely to be a blend.

Cotton blends are fine, however, if you plan to machine appliqué with a satin-stitch edge, because the edges do not need to be turned under. In fact, a permanent-press blend is often preferred, especially if the finished item will be washed repeatedly. A garment, for example, will come out of the dryer in great shape if the fabrics used for appliqué are blends of cotton-polyester.

I sometimes break the rules by using a fabric that is more "exotic," such as the gold lamé I used in the "Poinsettia" pattern on page 84. Precaution should be taken with these unusual fabrics—especially if you are a novice at quiltmaking. Velvets, for example, are really too thick to combine with cotton in these small Log Cabin blocks, yet, on occasion I have done just that. I think I have an ounce more rebel in me than purist! So go ahead and be creative but with a little bit of caution.

Fabric Preparation

Before using fabrics in these projects, prewash and tumble dry them. Anytime I purchase fabric, it goes directly to the laundry room before I add it to my studio shelves. Fabrics often shrink or "bleed," even though labeled preshrunk and colorfast. Even after washing, some dyes continue to bleed, so double-check by pressing a damp corner of the colored fabric onto a scrap of white fabric. If the fabric continues to "bleed," try to set the dye by adding 1 cup of white vinegar to a sink full of water and soaking the fabric. Rinse and test again. If the fabric continues to bleed, discard it. Press the prewashed and dried fabrics before starting to cut. Yardage requirements are based on 40 usable inches after preshrinking.

Fabric Selection

For Log Cabin picture designs, I use solids and small- to medium-scale prints that contain few colors. Very busy or large-scale prints tend to complicate the design and draw attention to themselves. It is best if the eye is drawn to the overall picture, rather than to a particularly busy or large-scale print within the picture. The strips used in these designs are very narrow and often, with a large multicolor print, the very color you wished to emphasize is not even contained in the strip. When this happens, you lose the color grouping and blur the picture you are trying to create.

Sometimes, I use all one fabric rather than a combination of fabrics. For example, in "Easter Parade," the bunny's vest is made up of strips cut from only one lavender fabric, and the chicks are composed of one yellow fabric for the body and one gold fabric for the wings. The resulting effect de-emphasizes the piecing and creates a unified look to the vest and chicks.

Color Groupings

Deciding which fabrics to include in each color group is very important. The groups should "read" as if they are a unit. For example, the shirt of the scarecrow in "Pumpkin Frost" is composed of several red fabrics. But they are similar in intensity and scale so they work together as a unit. The variety of fabrics is different enough to show off the piecing, yet not so different that the shirt looks choppy. The key is to achieve unity in intensity (darkness or lightness of a color) while combining fabrics that are slightly different so that all those little pieces show.

Also, you need to take into consideration the color groupings that surround the scarecrow's shirt—the pants and sky. The sky is a group of lights (beiges), and the pants are a group of mediums (lavenders), while the shirt "reads" as a dark. This enables all units of color to show well. If you place a group of medium greens next to a group of medium blues, they will blend together from a distance, and you will be in danger of losing your picture due to lack of contrast.

The following group of exercises will help you learn to group fabrics according to color and intensity (light, medium, and dark). Cut and paste ½"-wide strips of fabric onto the Bluebird Sample Quilt Plan found on the pullout pattern insert, using the color combination suggested. Try to aim for a unified look to the bird but one that contrasts with each background. Look at the finished sample from a distance. Did you achieve a clear picture of the bird, or are there strips that are too dark or too light? Are any of the prints too large or too busy? Is the bird distinctly different from the background? Think of these things as you select fabrics for the color groups in these patterns. Each color group could have from three to seven or even more fabrics. If you use only three fabrics, you will repeat the use of each fabric two or more times, which I do often.

To do a quick check of your color groups, lay out each color group, overlapping fabrics by ½" (the width of the finished strips in the patterns), then look at the group from a distance. If one of the fabrics stands out "like a sore thumb," discard it and use fewer fabrics.

Cutting and Pressing

Cutting

To make the blocks quickly and precisely, use a rotary cutter and mat. A good mat size is 18" x 24". The blocks are speed-pieced, using strips of fabric that are cut 1" wide. The only exception to this is the "Patsy Ann in Autumn" quilt, which has larger block centers. Read through each pattern before you begin to cut your 1"-wide strips, because some of the fabrics need to be reserved for appliqué pieces, borders, and binding strips.

The rotary cutter will easily cut through four to six layers of fabric. Use your quilter's ruler to measure and cut strips 1" wide. Be sure to make straight cuts that are perpendicular to the selvage; otherwise the strips might have a slight bias stretch. I usually fold my fabric only once (like it comes on the bolt) and cut strips selvage to selvage. You can stack two or three fabrics, each folded once. Try to avoid folding fabric too many times, since it will often result in crooked strips as shown below.

Folding like this:

can result in strips like this:

There is no need to mark fabrics for cutting; simply run the rotary cutter along the ruler edge. If the cut is not clean and the strip is still attached in spots, you probably have a nick in the blade; replace it with a fresh one. A rotary-cutter blade will last a long time if you avoid hitting the ruler and straight pins and if you clean and add a light coat of oil periodically. Be sure to wipe off any excess oil before cutting fabric.

Discard any strips that are wider or narrower than the rest, as they will result in blocks that are too small or too large. Use the same acrylic ruler throughout a project. I have found that ruler sizes vary, even though they all have 1" measurements.

If you must, you can mark strips and then cut with scissors, but cutting with a rotary cutter saves time and improves accuracy. It is well worth the initial investment.

As a general rule of thumb, it takes about 1 strip (1″ x 40′) to make one 13-piece block. One strip (1″ x 40′) will make 2 blocks if they have only 9 pieces. Using this guideline can help you figure the fabric required and the number of strips to cut. If the pattern calls for 12 blocks (13-piece blocks), you need 12″ of fabric or ⅓ yard. If the pattern calls for 12 blocks (9-piece blocks), you need 6″ of fabric or ⅙ yard.

Example: The pattern calls for 24 blocks (13-piece blocks) of sky blues. If you have only 1 blue fabric, you will need 24 strips. If you have 4 blue fabrics, you will need 6 strips of each. This formula makes it easy to figure yardage. In the above example, you would need a total of 24″ of fabric or ⅔ yard.

Pressing

With such narrow strips in these small Log Cabin blocks, it is essential to press each log as you go. Since my fingers are so close to the pressing, and steam is a bit more dangerous, I always use a dry iron, *not* a steam iron. Keep your ironing board close, since pressing is needed often during the piecing process.

I made a special free-standing board, which is just the right height, from an inexpensive wooden bar stool and a small wooden ironing board. I removed the short legs from the ironing board and screwed the ironing board to the top of the bar stool. (Screws go in underneath the bar stool and up into the wooden board.) The legs of the bar stool can be cut off at the desired height. Mine easily slides under my sewing table when not in use.

All seams in Log Cabin blocks are pressed away from the center square. When pressing the first double strip in the speed piecing process, press away from the strip that will be the center square of the blocks. As blocks progress in the speed-piecing process, always press seams toward the new uncut strip that has just been added. The wrong side of the block should look like this:

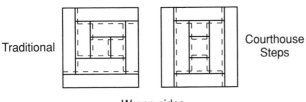

Traditional   Courthouse Steps

Wrong sides

It is also important to make sure there are no pleats or tucks. While the "logs" should not be stretched, they should be pressed all the

way out; otherwise the blocks will be too small. I always press on the right side (or top) of the blocks to prevent pleats and tucks.

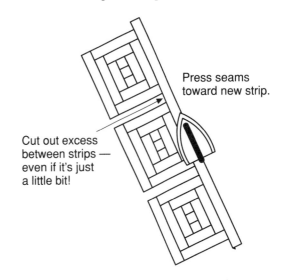

Press seams toward new strip.

Cut out excess between strips — even if it's just a little bit!

Many of my students have found it helpful to press seams while the blocks are still attached to the strip, before cutting blocks apart. This helps to keep blocks square as logs are added.

Templates

The templates on the following pages are shown full-size. Some of the blocks are Traditional Log Cabin blocks and some are Courthouse Steps blocks. There are also some unusual blocks: Off-Center, Split-Log, and Rounded Log Cabin blocks.

Traditional blocks are pieced in a clockwise order in all of my patterns, while some quilters piece their Traditional blocks in a counterclockwise sequence. Either way is correct, but for the patterns in this book, piece the blocks clockwise as shown. There are a few special blocks that require counterclockwise piecing. These are clearly indicated in the pattern section. Whenever you wish to divide a block in half diagonally, use a Traditional Block.

Be sure to add ¼″-wide seam allowances to each template. The pieces are numbered to indicate the order in which strips are added to the block. Some blocks are 9-piece blocks (a center square with 2 rounds of "logs" added). Some blocks are 13-piece blocks (a center square with 3 rounds of "logs" added). Some blocks are 17-piece blocks (a center square with 4 rounds of "logs" added).

Courthouse Steps is another type of Log Cabin Block. It is the easiest and least confusing of all the Log Cabin blocks to assemble.

Since the blocks are symmetrical, it is easy to see the strip placement during piecing. They are also quick to assemble. First, you speed up the beginning process by sewing three strips together instead of two strips as in other block types. (See page 13.) Second, as the block gets larger, you can sew the two opposite strips of fabric before pressing, which saves one pressing step. Whenever I have the option of using either type of block in a design, I choose Courthouse Steps. For example, in many of the background blocks that are all one color, I could use either type of block, but I always use Courthouse Steps.

There are also some special blocks. The **Off-Center Block** is used in two patterns. In "Tropical Fish," an Off-Center Block is created by sewing logs to only two sides of the center square. This leaves the center square (piece #1) bare on the other two sides.

The second Off-Center Block is used in "Autumn Roses." This block is created by sewing three logs onto two sides of the center square and only two logs on the remaining two sides, which creates an "off-center" look.

Another unusual block is the **Split-Log Block**. In this block, the center square is larger than normal, and the logs are pieced before being sewn to the block, giving them a "split" appearance. These blocks are used in the "Patsy Ann in Autumn" quilt.

The **Rounded Log Cabin Block** can be made from Traditional blocks or Courthouse Steps blocks. Cutting off four corners and adding a different fabric in the corners make the block appear "rounded." A pumpkin block in the "Haystack" pattern uses a Rounded Courthouse Steps Block.

The **Double-Rounded Log Cabin Block** is used in the "Amish Roses" pattern. These are rounded blocks with two rows of logs that have four corners cut off and replaced with triangles.

All of the blocks in this book can be made using the speed piecing methods discussed in the next chapter. It is much faster and easier than cutting individual templates. I suggest that you use the templates as guidelines for the piecing sequence and finished size. Remember, your assembled blocks will be squares that are ½" larger than the templates due to the ¼"-wide seam allowance all the way around. The template represents the finished size of the block after being sewn into the quilt.

Templates

Traditional Blocks

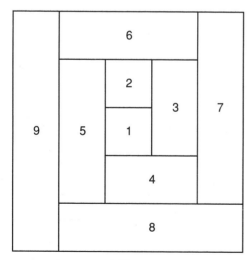

9 Piece
2½" finished / 3" unfinished

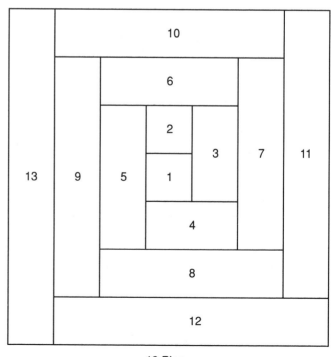

13 Piece
3½" finished / 4" unfinished

Traditional Block

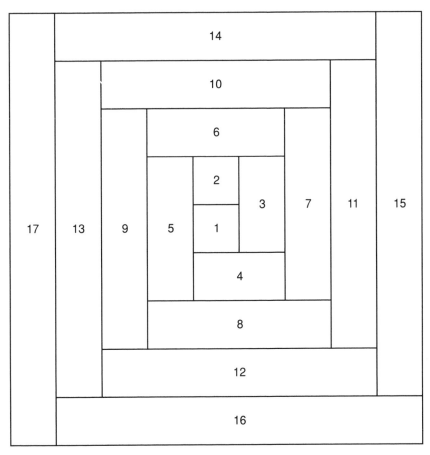

17 Piece
4½" finished / 5" unfinished

Courthouse Steps Blocks

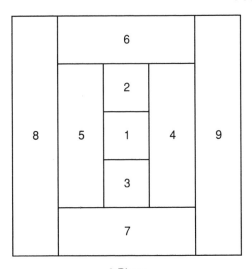

9 Piece
2½" finished / 3" unfinished

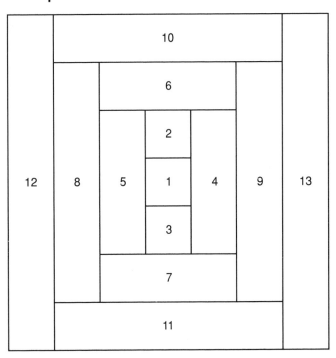

13 Piece
3½" finished / 4" unfinished

Off-Center Blocks

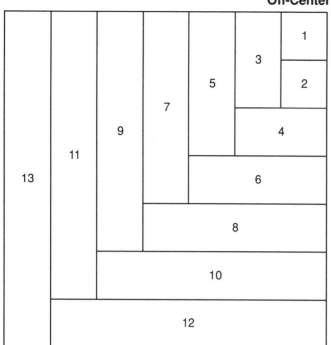

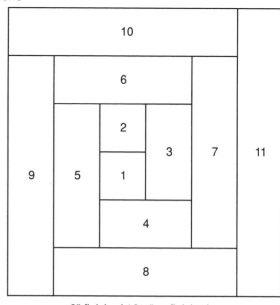

3½" finished / 4" unfinished

3" finished / 3½" unfinished

Split Log Block

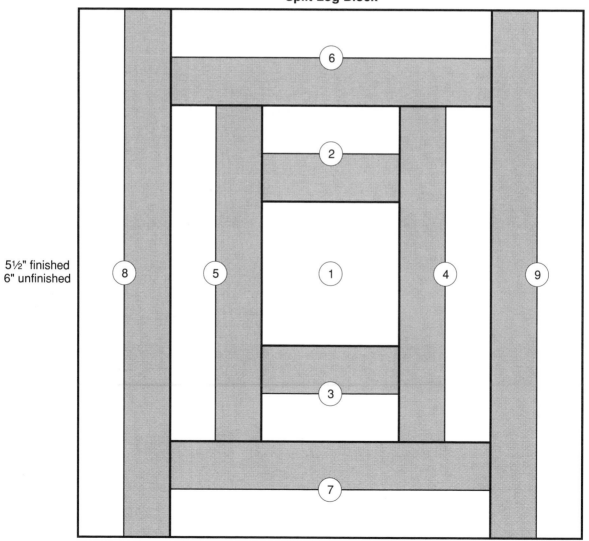

5½" finished
6" unfinished

Sew double logs, then piece like a regular Courthouse Steps block. Centers are cut 2" square.

Rounded Log Cabin Block (double rounded)

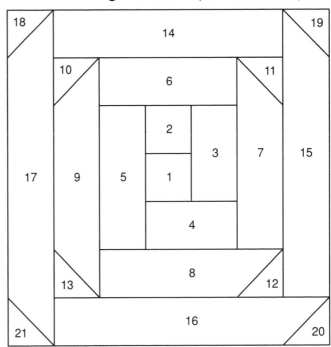

3½" finished / 4" unfinished

Rounded Courthouse Steps Block

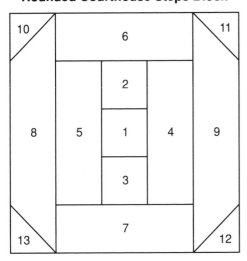

2½" finished / 3" unfinished

Speed Piecing

I recommend the use of speed piecing techniques for all of the projects in this book. There are usually several of each type and color combination of block, so making them all at once saves time.

Before beginning to speed-piece the blocks, it is a good idea to make a sample block. This will enable you to check strip width, seam allowances, and finished block size. *Use ¼"-wide seam allowances for all blocks.* If you have a special ¼" foot for your machine, use it. I know of one supplier who designed a special foot because of my first book, *Holiday Happenings.* Just make sure that there is never any fabric showing outside the ¼" foot as you sew. Line up the fabric along the edge of the foot.

When you have completed a sample block, compare it to the templates. Are your finished logs at least ½" wide? Check the center of the block. Is it a square? Have you pressed the logs all the way out or are there "pleats?" Is your block the right size? A 9-piece block should be 3" x 3" square including seam allowances; a 13-piece block should be 4" x 4" including seam allowances; and a 17-piece

block should be 5" x 5" including seam allowances.

Make the necessary adjustments and you are ready to begin speed piecing.

Basic Guidelines

- Cut selvages off of strips.
- Cut strips exactly 1" wide, straight, and accurate. Discard any strips that are crooked or too wide or too narrow.
- Use straight machine stitching with ¼"-wide seam allowances. Set machine at 12–14 stitches per inch and use a neutral-colored thread.
- Press strips after each sewing step.
- When cutting blocks apart, cut straight and perpendicular to the strip to keep blocks square.
- Do not change sewing machines, templates, or methods in the middle of a project. This may result in blocks of varying sizes.

Speed Piecing Traditional Blocks

The following sample exercise calls for six Traditional blocks.

Make 6 Traditional blocks
(½ browns, ½ whites)

Look at the Traditional Block. The smallest pieces are squares—the center (brown piece #1) and a piece beside the center (white piece #2). Cut an 8"-long strip from a 1"-wide strip of brown fabric and one of white fabric. This allows 1" of fabric for each block needed plus a couple of extra inches.

With right sides facing, sew the strips together along one edge, using a ¼"-wide seam allowance. Press seam away from the center color, in this case, brown.

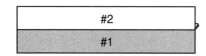

Press seams away
from center square (brown).

Cut the strip into 6 pieces, each 1" wide, using your ruler and rotary cutter or scissors. Now you have pieces #1 and #2 sewn together for all six blocks.

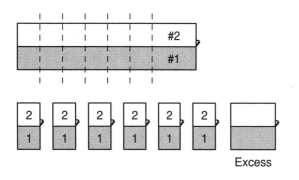

Excess

Piece #3 of the sample block is another white fabric. Choose a different white strip and lay this #3 strip on the machine with the right side facing up.

Note: With speed piecing, the new fabric strip always goes on the machine first and block pieces are laid on top of the strip.

Place the small block pieces, right side down, on top of the strip. Piece as shown with piece #1 at the top of the strip and piece #2 nearest you. Sew ¼" from the right-hand edge of the strip, adding blocks to the strip as you sew. You may butt the blocks together on the strip but do not overlap them.

Note: From this point on, graphs will not indicate fabric color, only the right and wrong sides of blocks and strips. The right side is darkened; the wrong side is not.

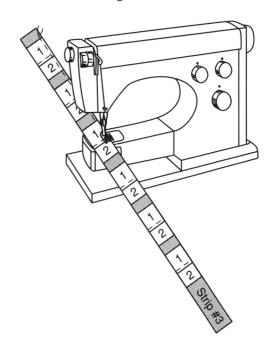

After sewing all six blocks to the strip, remove from the machine. Press the blocks with the seams toward the new uncut strip. Cut off excess and cut blocks apart with rotary cutter or scissors. If there is any fabric between blocks, cut this out! If small amounts of excess fabric are not removed, blocks will "grow." You now have six of these blocks.

Piece #4 is brown. Choose a different brown strip than piece #1 and place on the machine, right side up. Place the blocks on the strip with the right side down. Always keep the piece that you added to the block last (piece #3, in this case) nearest to you as you place it on the strip. Sew the blocks to the strip. Remove from the machine, press seams toward the new uncut strip, and cut blocks apart.

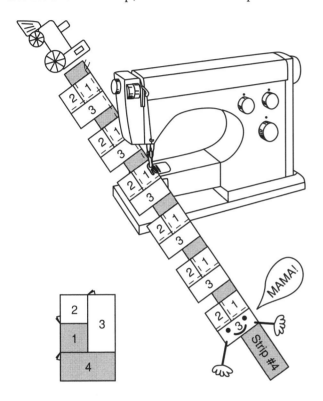

Repeat this process of sewing blocks to strips until all 9 pieces (or 13 or 17, depending on the pattern) have been added. Refer to the quilt plan for piece numbers and colors.

Some Helpful Hints

When working with the fabric strips and block pieces, think of the machine feed dog as a railroad track. Think of the long strips as the train and the blocks as the cargo. This helps you to remember that the strip (train) always goes on the machine (tracks) first and the cargo (blocks) are loaded onto the train. Never put the cargo under the train!

To remember how to place the blocks on the train, try to visualize this: The piece you added to the blocks last is your newest baby.

(He might be the biggest, but he is the newest!) Your newest baby always wants his mama. So place the blocks on the strip with the newest baby (latest strip addition) nearest you. He is near the caboose wanting to jump off the train to you.

I have found these little picture stories helpful for my students, but one frustrated New Jersey woman had the whole class in stitches when she groaned and loudly threatened to "throw Mama from the train!"

Speed Piecing Courthouse Steps Blocks

Look at the Courthouse Steps sample block. There are three small squares that are all the same size (pieces #1, #2, and #3). The sample exercise calls for four blocks, all blues. This means that you can use a variety of fabrics randomly placed.

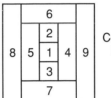

Courthouse Steps
Make 4 blocks
(all blues).

Select three blue strips, all different, and cut them 6″ long (1″ for each block needed plus a couple of extra inches). Sew the three strips together as shown and press seams away from the center strip.

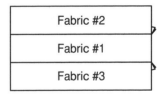

Press seams away from center strip.

Cut the strip into four pieces, each 1″ wide. You now have pieced #1, #2 and #3 for all four blocks.

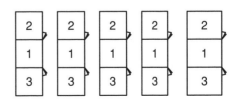

Excess

Select another blue strip for piece #4 (repeat a fabric if necessary). Lay the strip, right side up, on the machine. Place the blocks, right side down, on the strip. Unlike the Traditional blocks, you do not place the piece you added last nearest you. With Court-house Steps blocks, you must always place the blocks so that you will be sewing across a seam.

Select a blue strip for piece #5. Sew the blocks onto the strip as shown.

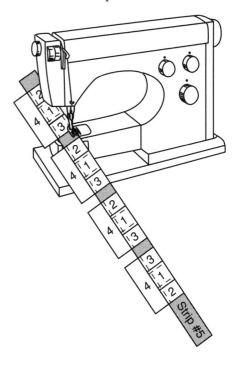

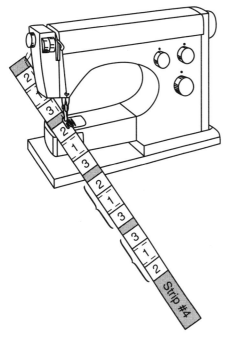

Blocks may be turned either way on the strip, with piece #2 or piece #3 at the top. Varying this placement will add more variety to your blocks. Butt the blocks together as you place them on the strip. Do not overlap the blocks. Sew ¼″ from the right-hand edge of the strip. Remove the blocks from the machine and press the seams toward the new, uncut strip. Cut blocks apart, removing any excess fabric between blocks. Your blocks will look like this:

Press seams toward the new, uncut strip, and cut blocks apart. Repeat this process of sewing blocks to the strips until all 9 pieces (or 13 or 17 pieces, depending on the pattern) have been added. Refer to the quilt plan regarding piece numbers and colors.

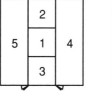

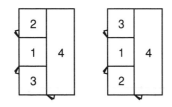

Speed piecing Off-Center Blocks

The sample exercise calls for five blocks, all greens. Look at the Off-Center Block. There are two squares (pieces #1 and #2) the same size.

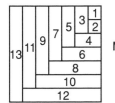

Make 5 blocks (all greens).

Cut two different 1″-wide green strips each about 7″ long (1″ for each block plus a couple of extra inches). Sew the strips together with right sides facing, using a ¼″-wide seam allowance. Press the seam away from strip #1. Cut the strip into five pieces, 1″ wide. You now have pieces #1 and #2 for all five blocks.

    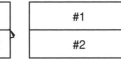

Excess

Lay another green strip on the machine. Place the blocks on the strip with piece #1 (center) at the top of the strip, and piece #2 nearest to you. Sew the blocks to the strip. Press seams toward the new, uncut strip. Cut blocks apart, making sure to remove any excess fabric between strips.

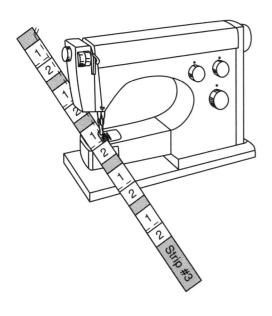

Lay a different green strip on the machine (repeat a fabric if necessary) and lay the blocks on the strip with piece #3 at the top of the strip, and the #1/#2 unit nearest to you. Sew blocks to the strip; press seams toward the new, uncut strip; cut blocks apart.

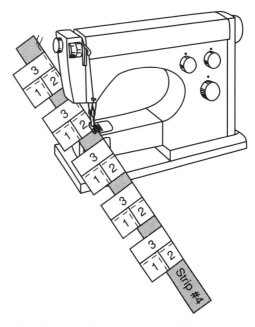

Continue adding strips to the block, making sure to add strips to only two sides of the block. This keeps piece #1 off-center, forming the Off-Center blocks. Add strips until the desired number is reached (9, 13, or 17).

Speed Piecing Rounded Log Cabin Blocks

These are started either as Traditional blocks or Courthouse Steps blocks. But at some point, either after 9 or 13 pieces have been added, four corners are cut off at 45° angles as shown.

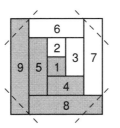 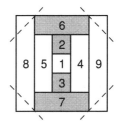

Cut off corners at a 45° angle.

These missing triangles must now be replaced with another color. Triangles could actually be cut and pieced in, but there is a speed-piecing technique that is much faster.

To Piece in the Triangles:

1. Make a paper template of the triangle to be removed.

Template for
cutting off corners

Tape the paper template to the edge of your ruler with the long edge of the triangle precisely aligned with the edge of the ruler. Use this guide on your ruler to cut off the corner of the square exactly.

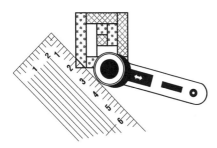

2. Lay the corner of the triangle over the corner of the square and cut along the long edge, using the edge of the ruler as the cutting guide. Cut off corners of blocks.

3. With right sides together, sew fabric strips at least 1″ wide onto corners as shown.

4. Press the new strips to the outside of block.

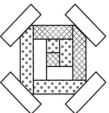

5. Trim off excess fabric, squaring up the block.

6. Continue adding strips as before, using the same fabric as you used for the triangles.

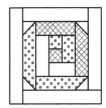

If you have several blocks to make using the same color triangles, place the blocks on the strip as shown. This will make one corner of each block. Press and cut blocks apart. Repeat this process with all blocks for each of the corners.

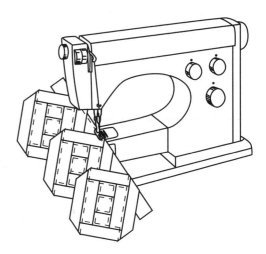

Sometimes the blocks are Double-Rounded blocks, as in the "Amish Roses" quilt. Make these blocks as Traditional blocks up through piece #9; then add four triangles. Add another round of logs and a second set of triangles.

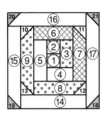

Double Rounded
Log Cabin Block

Speed Piecing Split-Log Blocks

Split-Log blocks are nothing more than regular blocks sewn with double strips. You could make a Traditional Split-Log Block, a Courthouse Steps Split-Log Block, even Off-Center or Rounded Split-Log blocks. The only difference is that the strip is a double strip.

"Patsy Ann in Autumn" (page 76) is the only pattern in this book that requires the Split-Log Block. It is slightly different because the center square is not made from 1″ strips, but from 2″ strips. It is a Courthouse Steps Split-Log Block. The center section (1, 2, 3) can be speed pieced. Start by sewing five long strips together before cutting the block sections.

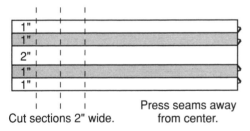

Cut sections 2" wide.   Press seams away from center.

Using double strips and following the procedure for Courthouse Steps shown on page 13, continue adding logs.

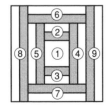

Speed Piecing Unusual Blocks

Sometimes a pattern calls for an unusual block. This means that the pieces might be added "out of order" from the normal piecing sequence. Or, there may be an extra piece added to a log. These are clearly illustrated and are always placed last in each pattern.

Block Assembly

Complete all of the individual blocks for a project before beginning to sew them together. (Each section of the "Easter Parade" and "Pumpkin Frost" quilts is considered an individual project.) When you are ready to sew the blocks together, follow the directions for each project to assemble blocks in horizontal or vertical rows.

When the rows are sewn together horizontally, press the seams between the blocks this way: row 1 to the right, row 2 to the left, row 3 to the right, and so forth. If rows are sewn vertically, press seams in row 1 up, seams in row 2 down, seams in row 3 up, and so forth. When you sew the rows together, the seams will meet and go in opposite directions.

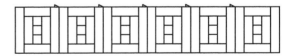

Row #1 - Press seams to right.

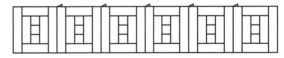

Row #2 - Press seams to left.

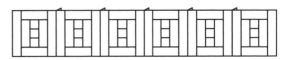

Row #3 - Press seams to right.

Always match blocks at the connecting seam between them. If blocks do not match exactly, ease the larger block to fit the smaller block. If there is too much difference for them to match, you may have to adjust or even remake a block. The long seams between rows may be pressed in either direction.

Appliqué

Appliqué is the "application" or attachment of a piece of fabric to a background fabric. The background may be pieced or it may be a solid piece. Appliqué can be done by hand or by machine. For the latest methods in machine appliqué, I suggest buying or borrowing a good book on the subject. There are many new products and techniques now available that make machine work look like you have done hours of handwork. For the quilts in this book, I have used primarily hand techniques.

I use so many different appliqué methods that it is difficult to choose one "best technique." In one quilt, I often use three different techniques because each has its own advantages and special uses.

Hand Appliqué - Method 1 - Basted

This is the method I use most often because it is fairly fast and allows me to have some control over the pieces to be appliquéd.

1. Place the traced patterns onto a light box and, using a marking tool of your choice, trace the patterns and embroidery lines onto the right side of the appropriate fabrics. As you mark the fabric, be sure to leave space for ¼"-wide seam allowances around each piece.
2. Cut out each piece of fabric, adding ¼"-wide seam allowances to all edges as you cut. This ¼" need not be marked or exact. Fold the seam allowance to the wrong side of each piece exactly on the drawn line, but do not let pencil lines show.
3. Using a single-knotted basting thread, baste with running stitches around the folded edges of the fabric. (I like to use quilting thread for basting because it is strong and will pull out later without breaking.) Keep the knot on the right side of the fabric so that the basting thread is easy to remove when the appliqué is complete.

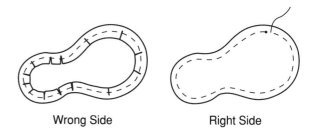

Wrong Side   Right Side

Clip curves to fold if necessary.   No need to knot end

4. Pin or baste appliqué pieces to the background fabric. I baste only if the appliqué is large or irregular in shape.
5. Using a small, very thin needle (called a sharp) and a single, matching thread with one end knotted, appliqué. Use a blind stitch as shown below.

Blind stitch

Hand Appliqué - Method 2 - Freezer Paper

I find this method works best for appliquéing small, perfect circles, leaves, or any small piece that is repeated numerous times and is expected to look exactly the same.

There are several variations of the freezer-paper method. I use the following.

1. Trace the reverse of each pattern piece onto the uncoated side of the freezer paper. (For circles and most leaves, the reverse would be the same, of course.)
2. Cut out the pieces of paper on the marked line. Press the paper pieces with coated side down to the wrong side of the appropriate fabrics. Cut fabric pieces ¼" larger than the paper pattern all around.
3. Pin the pieces in place as you appliqué and use the needle to turn the raw edges under. The freezer paper works as a stabilizer and creates neat, rounded edges.
4. Appliqué pieces using a blind stitch. When the appliqué is complete, slit the background fabric behind the appliquéd piece and remove the freezer paper. If the freezer paper is large and well adhered to the fabric, use a

manicurist's orange stick to loosen it and tweezers to pull it out through the slit fabric.

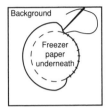

Press paper to fabric.

Use the needle to push raw edges under freezer paper.

Hand Appliqué - Method 3 - Paper Patch

One of the oldest methods used to get nice, smooth-edged circles is the paper-patch method. Trace the pattern pieces onto heavy bond paper and cut them out.

1. Cut appropriate fabric pieces ¼″ larger than the paper patterns.
2. With a single, knotted thread, sew a running stitch around the edges of the fabric piece.

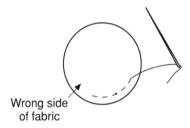

3. Place the paper pattern next to the wrong side of the fabric piece. Pull stitches taut around paper.

Knot the end and press with paper inside.

4. Remove the paper and proceed to appliqué. Or appliqué first and then slit the background fabric to remove paper when the appliqué is complete. Remove paper with tweezers.

Hand Appliqué - Method 4 - Stitch and Turn

This method is helpful for those who suffer from arthritis or who feel "all thumbs" when trying hand appliqué. It is also useful for small, irregularly shaped pieces.

1. Mark patterns and fabrics as in the basted method, with one exception: mark fabrics on the wrong side and omit the embroidery lines until later. Cut pieces ¼″ larger than the pattern lines indicate.
2. Use a nonfusible, lightweight interfacing to back the fabric pieces. Cut the interfacing slightly larger than the cut fabric piece. Place the right side of the fabric against the interfacing and machine stitch around the piece on the solid pencil lines.

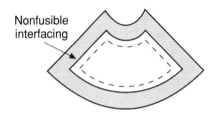

Trim the interfacing to match the fabric piece, clipping curves if necessary.

3. Cut a small slash in the center of the interfacing and turn the piece right side out. Use a manicurist's orange stick to help turn it, if necessary. Press. Using a light table and a marking tool of your choice, mark the embroidery lines; appliqué as instructed in Method 1.

Broderie Perse

Broderie Perse means "Persian embroidery." It is actually an appliqué technique, although embroidery is often added. The roses in the "Autumn Roses" quilt have been appliquéd using this method. Flowers, birds, or fruit are cut from the fabric's printed design, but with ¼″-wide seam allowance added to the edges to be turned under. This edge can be prebasted, but more often, the pieces are simply pinned to the fabric and the edges are turned under with the needle as you go. This is sometimes called "needle-under" appliqué.

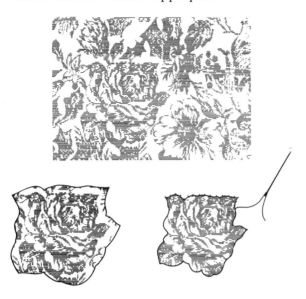

Embroidery

Always use good-quality embroidery floss and small embroidery needles. I often use a size 10 quilting needle. The smaller the needle, the finer the stitch you will achieve.

A good embroidery hoop to hold the fabric taut is a must. I prefer the plastic type with metal spring used for machine embroidery.

Use two strands of floss (never three) for most embroidery. For small details, such as lips and eyelashes, or for dates and signatures, I use one strand to get a neater, more delicate embroidered line.

Although there are entire books filled with the various embroidery stitches, I have included only those necessary for the patterns in this book.

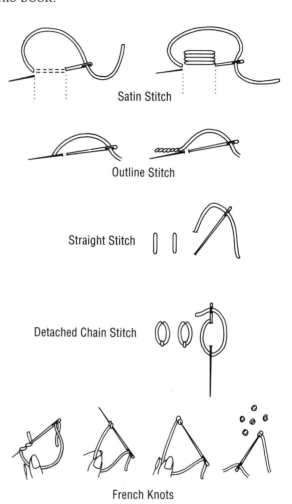

PATTERNS

Fourteen seasonal quilt patterns are included in this book. Two of the quilts, "Easter Parade" and "Pumpkin Frost," are collage quilts made up of several smaller designs. That makes a total of twenty-nine fun projects to take you through the year.

Each time you start a new project, it is a good idea to review the general guidelines. I recommend coloring the quilt plans and the individual blocks to use as a guide as you are piecing.

Full-sized templates are included on pages 8–11. Use these as a size guide for finished blocks, as well as a piecing sequence guide. If a pattern contains unusual blocks that require a different piecing sequence, they will be clearly identified in each pattern.

Appliqué and embroidery are added after the blocks are sewn together. Appliqué templates on the pullout pattern inserts are full size, but you will need to add ¼″-wide seam allowances.

Finishing techniques for all of the projects are found on pages 86–88.

SPRING

EASTER PARADE

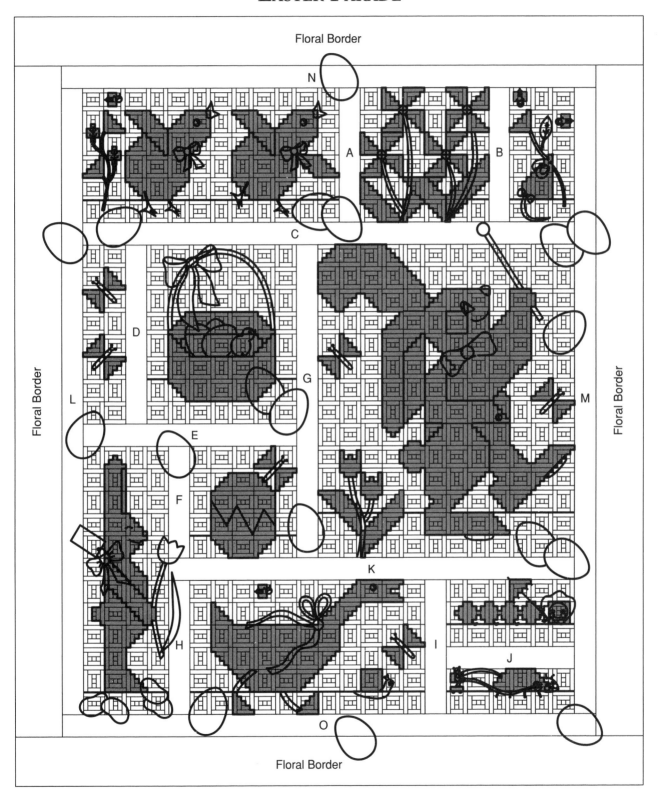

Floral Border

Floral Border

Floral Border

Floral Border

N

A

B

C

D

G

L

E

M

F

H

I

J

K

O

General directions for all of the Easter Parade patterns:

1. Make a sample 9-piece block to check measurements and seam allowances. The sample block should be 3″ x 3″ square, unfinished, and 2½″ x 2½″ square, finished, after assembling the quilt.
2. Fabric requirements for individual sections of this quilt do not include fabric for borders or backing. Fabric requirements and finishing instructions for the entire "Easter Parade" quilt begin below.

Color Photo: page 36

Size: Approximately 74″ x 86½″
535 Blocks (9-piece blocks)

Finished Block Size: 2½″ x 2½″

Materials:

Yardage requirements below are for making all 11 sections of the Easter Parade quilt. If you wish to make only an individual section of this quilt, refer to the yardage requirements given with the directions for that section.

Note: For more variety, use an assortment of fabrics for any of the single colors listed.

4⅛ yds. assorted blues for sky
1½ yds. assorted light greens for grass
1 yd. yellow for chicks, caterpillar, and eggs
¾ yd. assorted whites for bunny, duck, and flower
½ yd. assorted beiges for bunny and duck's wing
⅓ yd. dark pink for flower, bow, ladybug, eggs, and butterflies
¼ yd. purple for bunny's vest and eggs
¼ yd. pink for eggs, bunny's cheek, and flower
⅛ yd. orange for eggs, duck's feet, and bill
⅛ yd. dark green for leaves
⅛ yd. gold for chicks' wings and butterflies' bodies
3″ x 40″ strip of medium green for leaves
Scraps of spring colors for eggs and other appliqué pieces
Scrap of black for eyes
2 yds. floral print for border and binding
1½ yds. green for sashing
4½ yds. for backing

Notions: green bias tape;
black, white, brown, gold, orange, pink, and green embroidery floss

Directions for Finishing

1. Make all 11 sections of the quilt (pages 23 – 35). (See "General directions for all of the Easter Parade patterns," opposite.)
2. Cut 3″-wide strips for sashing; crosscut strips into the following sections, piecing as necessary to the required length. Measurements are based on finished blocks of 2½″ x 2½″. Adjust measurements for sashing strips accordingly, if your blocks are a different size.
   A, B, H, I, J - each 3″ x 15½″
   C - 3″ x 58″
   D - 3″ x 20½″
   E - 3″ x 25½″
   F - 3″ x 13″
   G - 3″ x 35½″
   K - 3″ x 48″
   L, M - each 3″ x 70½″
   N, O - each 3″ x 63″
3. Using the quilt plan on page 21 as a guide, sew sashing to the quilt sections in the following order. Do not stretch the sashing as you sew it to the pieced sections; otherwise it will not fit the next section of pieced blocks.
   a. Sew sashings "A" and "B" between chicks, flowers, and mouse.
   b. Sew sashing "C" to bottom of chick/flower/mouse section.
   c. Sew sashing "D" between butterflies and basket.
   d. Sew sashing "F" between top of chocolate bunny and Easter egg.
   e. Sew sashing "E" between butterfly/basket and chocolate bunny/egg.
   f. Sew sashing "G" to left side of marching bunny.
   g. Sew sashing "J" between caterpillar and ladybug.
   h. Sew sashing "I" between duck and caterpillar/ladybug.
   i. Sew sashing "H" to left side of duck/caterpillar/ladybug.
   j. Sew sashing "K" to top of duck/caterpillar/ladybug.
   k. Sew chocolate bunny/basket section to marching bunny along sashing "G."
   l. Sew chick/flower/mouse section to top of bunnies/baskets along sashing "C."
   m. Piece remaining duck section into quilt along sashings "H" and "K."
   n. Sew sashings "L" and "M" to sides of quilt.
   o. Sew sashings "N" and "O" to top and bottom of quilt.
4. Cut floral borders 6″ wide and sew to sides, top, and bottom of quilt. Corners may be mitered if desired. (See page 86.)
5. Using the baton, jelly bean, and egg tem-

plates, T-4, T-5, and T-9, on the pullout pattern inserts, appliqué pieces to quilt, across sashing, and into borders as shown. Check for a good color balance of eggs.

6. Embroider any desired names on eggs, using black embroidery floss.

7. Mark top for quilting.

8. Layer quilt top, batting, and backing; quilt.

9. Bind edges with straight strips of fabric, as shown on page 88.

CATERPILLAR

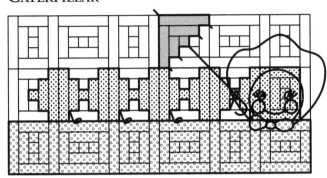

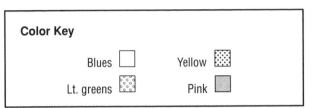

Color Key

Blues ☐   Yellow ▨

Lt. greens ▨   Pink ▨

Traditional Blocks

Make 1
Pink & blue/Umbrella

Courthouse Steps Blocks

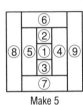

Make 6
Lt. green/Grass

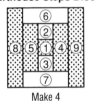

Make 5
Blue/Sky

Make 4
Yellow & blue/Caterpillar

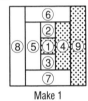

Make 1
Blue & yellow/Tail

Make 1
Yellow & blue/Head

Color Photo: page 36

Size: 15½″ x 8″

18 Blocks (9-piece blocks)

Finished Block Size: 2½″ x 2½″

Materials: 44″-wide fabric

⅛ yd. assorted blues for sky
⅛ yd. assorted light greens for grass
⅛ yd. yellow for caterpillar
Scraps of the following:
    Pink for umbrella
    Dark pink for bonnet
    Aqua for bow

Notions: black, white, and pink embroidery floss

Directions

1. Color in the quilt plan and blocks with colored pencils to help eliminate mistakes.

2. Using either the speed-piecing method or templates, make the blocks shown above.

3. When all the blocks are completed, sew the blocks together in horizontal rows as shown in the quilt plan above. Then sew the rows together, making sure to match the seams between each block.

4. Using the templates, T-7 Caterpillar on the pullout pattern insert, appliqué the dark pink bonnet and aqua bow to the blocks.

5. Complete embroidery:

    legs—black outline stitch
    mouth and eyelashes—black outline stitch
    center of bow—black outline stitch
    umbrella handle—black outline stitch
    eyes—black satin stitch
    cheeks and feet—pink satin stitch
    "gleam" in caterpillar's eyes—white satin stitch
    points on umbrella—black straight stitches

6. This section is now ready to add to the entire quilt or to finish as an individual project.

7. For individual project:
    a. Add borders as desired.
    b. Layer quilt top, batting, and backing; quilt.
    c. Bind edges with straight strips of fabric, as shown on page 88.

FLOWERS

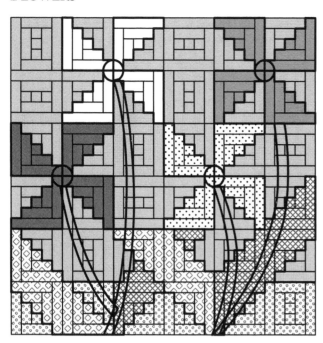

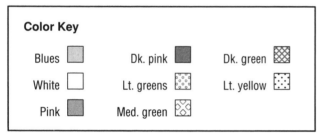

Traditional Blocks

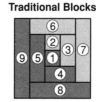

Make 4
Pink & blue/Flower

Make 4
Dk. pink & blue/Flower

Make 4
Yellow and blue/Flower

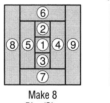

Make 4
White & blue/Flower

Make 3
Med. green & lt. green/
Leaves

Make 3
Dk. green & blue/
Leaves

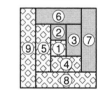

Make 2
Dk. green & lt. green/
Leaves

Make 2
Med. green, dk. green
& blue/Leaves

Make 1
Med. green & blue/Leaf

Color Key

Blues	▨	Dk. pink	■
White	□	Lt. greens	⬚
Pink	▨	Med. green	⬚
		Dk. green	⬚
		Lt. yellow	⬚

Courthouse Steps Blocks

Make 8
Blue/Sky

Make 1
Lt. green/Grass

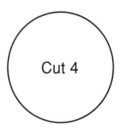

Cut 4

Flower Center
(Gold)

Color Photo: page 36

Size: 15½" x 15½"

36 Blocks (9-piece blocks)

Finished Block Size: 2½" x 2½"

Materials: 44"-wide fabric

⅓ yd. assorted blues for sky
Scraps of assorted light greens for grass*
Scraps of the following*:
    Medium green for leaves
    Dark green for leaves
    White for flower
    Light yellow for flower
    Pink for flower
    Dark pink for flower
Scrap of gold for flower centers
You must be able to cut 1"-wide strips from these scraps.

Notions: green bias tape for flower stems

Directions

1. Color in the quilt plan and blocks with colored pencils to help eliminate mistakes.
2. Using either the speed-piecing method or templates, make the blocks shown above.
3. When all the blocks are completed, sew the blocks together in horizontal rows as shown in the quilt plan above. Then sew the rows together, making sure to match the seams between each block.
4. Appliqué flower stems, using green bias tape, as shown in the quilt plan.
5. Using the freezer-paper method (page 18), appliqué the gold flower centers to the flowers.
6. This section is now ready to add to the entire quilt or to finish as an individual project.
7. For individual project:
   a. Add borders as desired.
   b. Layer quilt top, batting, and backing; quilt.
   c. Bind edges with straight strips of fabric, as shown on page 88.

BASKET

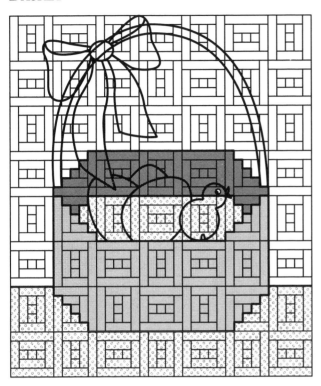

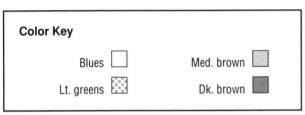

Traditional Blocks

Make 2
Med. brown &
lt. green/Basket

Make 2
Dk. brown & blue/
Basket

Make 1
Med. brown, dk. brown
& lt. green/Basket

Courthouse Steps Blocks

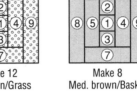

Make 12
Lt. green/Grass

Make 8
Med. brown/Basket

Special Block
*Note reverse
piecing sequence.

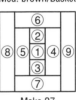

Make 1
Med. brown, dk. brown
& lt. green/Basket

Make 3
Dk. brown/Basket

Make 27
Blue/Sky

Color Key

Blues	☐	Med. brown	▨
Lt. greens	▨	Dk. brown	■

Color Photo: page 36

Size: 18″ x 20½″
56 Blocks (9-piece blocks)

Finished Block Size: 2½″ x 2½″

Materials: 44″-wide fabric
½ yd. assorted blues for sky
¼ yd. assorted light greens for grass
¼ yd. medium brown for basket
⅛ yd. dark brown for inner basket
⅛ yd. dark pink for bow
Scrap of yellow for chick
Scraps of various colors for eggs

Notions: orange, black, brown, and white embroidery floss

Directions

1. Color in the quilt plan and blocks with colored pencils to help eliminate mistakes.
2. Using either the speed-piecing method or templates, make the blocks shown above.

Notice that one of the Basket blocks has a reverse piecing sequence.

3. When all the blocks are completed, sew the blocks together in horizontal rows as shown in the quilt plan above. Then sew the rows together, making sure to match the seams between each block.
4. Using the templates, T-3 Basket on the pull-out pattern insert, complete appliqué:

   medium brown handle to basket (adjust handle to fit)
   pink bow to handle
   colored eggs as shown in quilt plan
   yellow chick to top of basket

5. Complete embroidery:

   bow—brown outline stitch
   chick's legs and beak—orange satin stitch
   eye—black satin stitch
   "gleam" in chick's eye—white satin stitch

6. This section is now ready to add to the entire quilt or to finish as an individual project.
7. For individual project:
   a. Add borders as desired.
   b. Layer quilt top, batting, and backing; quilt.
   c. Bind edges with straight strips of fabric, as shown on page 88.

Bunny

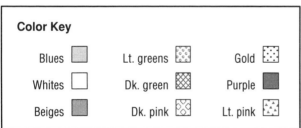

Color Key

Blues	Lt. greens	Gold
Whites	Dk. green	Purple
Beiges	Dk. pink	Lt. pink

Color Photo: page 36

Size: 30½″ x 35½″

168 Blocks (9-piece blocks)

Finished Block Size: 2½″ x 2½″

Traditional Blocks

Make 12
Beige & blue/Bunny

Make 6
White & blue/Bunny

Make 4
Dk. green & lt. green/
Leaves

Make 3
Dk. green & blue/
Leaves

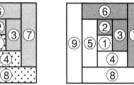

Make 4
Gold & blue/Butterflies

Make 2
White & beige/Bunny

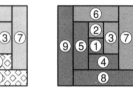

Make 1
Dk. pink & blue/Ear

Make 1
Purple & beige/Vest

Make 1
Dk. pink & white/Ear

Make 1
Purple & blue/Vest

Make 1
White, beige & blue/
Bunny

Make 1
White & lt. green/
Bunny foot

Make 1
White, beige & blue/
Bunny

Courthouse Steps Blocks

Make 55
Blue/Sky

Make 29
White/Bunny

Make 16
Lt. green/Grass

Make 11
Beige/Bunny

Make 4
Blue & white/Sky

Make 4
Purple/Vest

Make 2
Dk. pink/Ears

Make 2
Dk. pink & blue/Tulips

Make 2
Blue & dk. pink/Tulips

Make 1
Blue & white/Tip of ear

Make 1
Beige & blue/Bunny

Make 1
White & purple/
Bunny & vest

Make 1
White & blue/Bunny

Make 1
Lt. pink/Cheeks

Materials: 44″-wide fabric

1 yd. assorted blues for sky
½ yd. assorted whites for bunny
⅓ yd. assorted beiges for bunny
¼ yd. assorted light greens for grass
⅛ yd. dark pink for ears, flowers, nose, foot
   pads, bow tie
⅛ yd. purple for vest
3″ x 40″ strip of dark green for leaves
3″ x 40″ strip of gold for butterflies and baton
Scrap of light pink for cheeks
Scrap of yellow for butterflies' bodies
Scrap of black for eye

Notions: green bias tape for flower stems;
   black and white embroidery floss

Directions

1. Color in the quilt plan and blocks with colored pencils to help eliminate mistakes.
2. Using either the speed-piecing method or templates, make the blocks shown on page 26 and at left.
3. When all the blocks are completed, sew the blocks together in horizontal rows as shown in the quilt plan on page 26. Then sew the rows together, making sure to match the seams between each block.
4. Using the templates, T-4 Bunny on the pullout pattern insert, complete appliqué:

   tooth to bunny
   bow tie to bunny
   gold butterfly bodies to butterfly blocks
   black eye to head
   dark pink nose to head
   dark pink footpads to bottom of feet
   yellow button to vest
   green bias tape stems to flowers

5. Complete embroidery:

   butterflies' antennae—black outline stitch
   button thread—black outline stitch
   bunny's mouth and eyelashes—black
      outline stitch
   tips of antennae—black French knots
   "gleam" in bunny's eye—white satin stitch

6. This section is now ready to add to the entire quilt or to finish as an individual project.
7. For individual project:
   a. Add borders as desired. Appliqué gold baton after borders have been added.
   b. Layer quilt top, batting, and backing; quilt.
   c. Bind edges with straight strips of fabric, as shown on page 88.

CHOCOLATE BUNNY

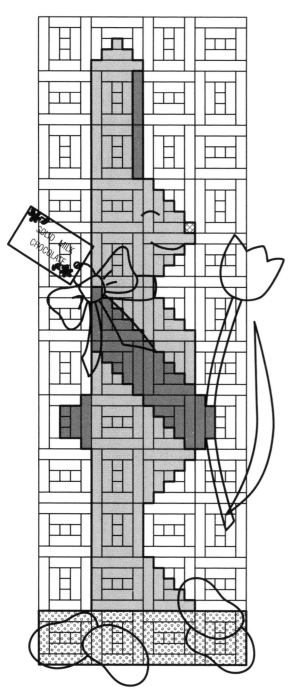

Color Key

Blues ☐		Lt. greens ▨		Dk. brown ■	
Pink ⊠		Med. browns ▨			

Color Photo: page 36

Size: 10½″ x 30½″

48 Blocks (9-piece blocks)

Finished Block Size: 2½″ x 2½″

Traditional Blocks

Make 4
Med. brown & blue/
Bunny

Make 4
Dk. brown & med.
brown/Bunny

Courthouse Steps Blocks

Make 24
Blue/Sky

Make 6
Med. brown/Bunny

Make 4
Lt. green/Grass

Make 2
Med. brown &
dk. brown/Ears

Make 1
Med. brown & blue/
Tip of ear

Make 1
Blue & dk. brown/
Hand

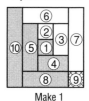

Make 1
Blue & dk. brown/Tail

Special Block

*Note piecing
sequence.
Sew #8 to #9,
then add to block.

Make 1

Materials: 44″-wide fabric

½ yd. assorted blues for sky

¼ yd. assorted medium browns for bunny

Scraps of assorted dark browns for bunny*

Scraps of assorted light greens for grass*

Scraps of the following:

    Pink for bow and nose

    Yellow for tulip

    Orange, lavender, purple, and dark pink
      for jelly beans

    White for tag

    Dark green for leaf

*You must be able to cut 1″-wide strips from
these scraps.

Notions: green bias tape for flower stem; brown, pink, green, and black embroidery floss

Directions

1. Color in the quilt plan and blocks with colored pencils to help eliminate mistakes.
2. Using either the speed piecing method or templates, make the blocks shown on page 28.
3. When all the blocks are completed, sew the blocks together in vertical rows as shown in the quilt plan on page 28. Then sew the rows together, making sure to match the seams between each block.
4. Using the templates, T-5 Chocolate Bunny on the pullout pattern insert, complete appliqué:

   green bias tape stem to blocks
   yellow tulip to blocks
   green leaf to stem

pink neckband and bow at neck
white tag to blocks above bow
various colored jelly beans as shown in quilt plan

5. Complete embroidery:

   eyes and mouth— black outline stitch
   string on tag—black outline stitch
   "solid milk chocolate" and lines in bow— brown outline stitch
   daisies on tag—pink and green lazy-daisy stitches; green outline-stitched stems

6. This section is now ready to add to the entire quilt or to finish as an individual project.
7. For individual project:
   a. Add borders as desired.
   b. Layer quilt top, batting, and backing; quilt.
   c. Bind edges with straight strips of fabric, as shown on page 88.

LADYBUG

Color Key

Blues □   Lt. greens ▨   Dk. pink ▨

Beige ▨   Dk. brown ▪   Gold ▨

Brown ▨

Color Photo: page 36

Size: 15½″ x 5½″

12 Blocks (9-piece blocks)

Finished Block Size: 2½″ x 2½″

Courthouse Steps Blocks

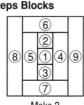

Make 6
Lt. green/Grass

Make 2
Blue/Sky

Special Blocks Courthouse Steps

Make 1
Dk. pink & dk. brown/
Ladybug

Piece as a normal Courthouse Steps except sew #6, #7 & #8 together before adding to block.

Make 1
Blue, gold, beige & brown/Bee in wagon

*Note change of piecing sequence from regular Courthouse Steps.

Special Blocks Traditional

Make 1
Dk. pink, dk. brown
& blue/Ladybug

Piece as a regular Traditional Block except: Sew #8 to #9, then add to block. Sew #10 to #11, then add to block.

Make 1
Dk. pink, dk. brown
& blue/Ladybug

Piece as a regular Traditional Block except sew #9, #10 & #11 together before adding to block.

Materials: 44″-wide fabric

⅛ yd. assorted light greens for grass

Scraps of assorted blues for sky*

3″ x 40″ strip of dark pink for ladybug

Scrap pieces of the following:

> Dark brown for ladybug's spots
> Gold for bee
> Beige for bee's wings
> Pink for ladybug's face
> Lavender for ribbon
> Brown for bee's wagon

You must be able to cut 1"-wide strips from these scraps.

Notions: black, pink, white, green, and brown embroidery floss

Directions

1. Color in the quilt plan and blocks with colored pencils to help eliminate mistakes.
2. Using either the speed-piecing method or templates, make the blocks shown on page 29. Notice the special piecing of the ladybug blocks and the bee in the wagon block.
3. When all the blocks are completed, sew the blocks together in horizontal rows as shown in the quilt plan on page 29. Then sew the rows together, making sure to match the seams between each block.

4. Using the templates, T-8 Ladybug on the pullout pattern insert, complete appliqué:

> *lavender ribbons* to blocks
> *pink ladybug's head* to blocks
> *yellow bee's head* to top of bee's body

Use the freezer-paper method of appliqué, page 18, for the heads.

5. Complete embroidery:

> *bee's legs*—black outline stitch
> *bee's eyes and antennae tips*—black French knots
> *bee's bow tie and shoes*—pink satin stitch
> *ladybug's cheeks and antennae*—pink satin stitch
> *wagon wheels*—brown satin stitch
> *ladybug's eyes*—white and green satin stitch
> *ladybug's eyelashes*—brown outline stitch
> *ladybug's nostrils*—pink French knots
> *ladybug's legs*—double rows of brown outline stitch

6. This section is now ready to add to the entire quilt or to finish as an individual project.
7. For individual project:
   a. Add borders as desired.
   b. Layer quilt top, batting, and backing; quilt.
   c. Bind edges with straight strips of fabric, as shown on page 88.

Duck

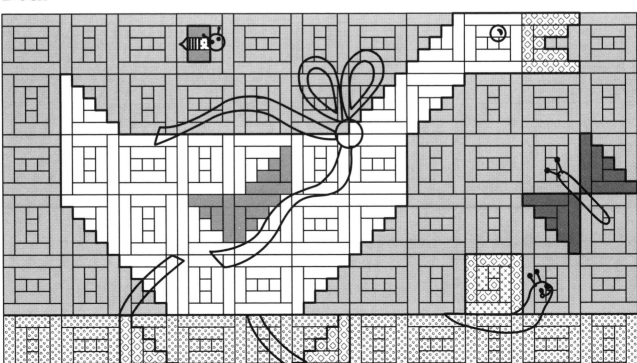

Color Key

Blues Orange Yellow

Whites Lt. greens Gold

Beige Dk. pink

Color Photo: page 36

Size: 28″ x 15½″
66 Blocks (9-piece blocks)

Finished Block Size: 2½″ x 2½″

Traditional Blocks

Make 8
White & blue/Duck

Make 3
White & beige/Wing

Make 2
Dk. pink & blue/
Butterfly

Make 2
Orange & lt. green/
Feet

Courthouse Steps Blocks

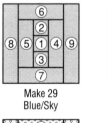

Make 29
Blue/Sky

Make 10
White/Duck

Make 9
Lt. green/Grass

Make 1
Orange & blue/Beak

Special Blocks

Make 1
Orange & yellow/Snail

*Note reverse
piecing sequence.

Make 1
Blue, gold &
beige/Bee

See Bee template
on pullout pattern
insert, T-1 Chicks

Materials: 44″-wide fabric

½ yd. assorted blues for sky
¼ yd. assorted whites for duck
¼ yd. assorted light greens for grass and
 butterfly's body
⅛ yd. yellow for snail and bow
3″ x 40″ strip of beige for duck's wing and
 bee's wings
3″ x 40″ strip of orange for snail shell, duck's
 feet, and bill
Scraps of the following:
 Dark pink for butterfly's body
 Gold for bee body
 Black for duck's eye

Notions: white, black, and pink embroidery
 floss

Directions

1. Color in the quilt plan and blocks with colored pencils to help eliminate mistakes.
2. Using either the speed-piecing method or templates, make the blocks shown at left.
3. When all the blocks are completed, sew the blocks together in horizontal rows as shown in the quilt plan on page 30. Then sew the rows together, making sure to match the seams between each block.
4. Using the template, T-6 Duck on the pullout pattern insert, complete appliqué:

    orange legs to duck
    yellow bow to neck of duck
    yellow snail body to snail block
    light green butterfly body to butterfly block
    yellow bee's head to end of bee's body
    black duck's eye to head

    Use the freezer-paper method, page 18, to appliqué small round pieces.
5. Complete embroidery:

    all sets of antennae—black outline stitch
     with French knot tips
    bee's eyes—black French knots
    bee's stripes—black outline stitch
    snail's eyes—black satin stitch
    snail's cheeks—pink satin stitch
    snail's mouth—black outline stitch
    "gleam" in duck's eye—white satin stitch

6. This section is now ready to add to the entire quilt or to finish as an individual project.
7. For individual project:
    a. Add borders as desired.
    b. Layer quilt top, batting, and backing; quilt.
    c. Bind edges with straight strips of fabric, as shown on page 88.

EASTER EGG

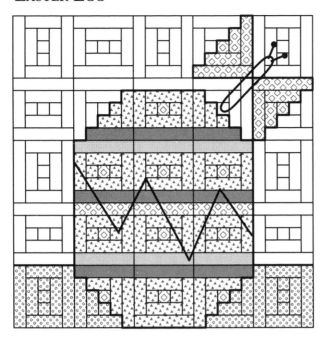

Color Key

Blues ☐   Lt. greens ▨   Purple ■

Yellow ▨   Dk. pink ▨   Orange ▨

Color Photo: page 36

Size: 13″ x 13″
25 Blocks (9-piece blocks)

Finished Block Size: 2½″ x 2½″

Materials: 44″-wide fabric
¼ yd. assorted blues for sky
⅛ yd. yellow for egg
Scraps of assorted light greens for grass*
Scraps of the following:*
    Dark pink for butterfly
    Purple, orange, and dark pink for egg
    Gold for butterfly's body
You must be able to cut 1″-wide strips from these scraps.

Notions: brown and black embroidery floss

Directions

1. Color in the quilt plan and blocks with colored pencils to help eliminate mistakes.
2. Using either the speed-piecing method or templates, make the blocks shown at left.
3. When all the blocks are completed, sew the blocks together in horizontal rows as indicated in the quilt plan above. Then sew the rows together, making sure to match the seams between each block.
4. Using the template, T-6 Duck on the pullout pattern insert, appliqué the butterfly's body to the butterfly blocks.
5. Complete embroidery:

    jagged line through egg—brown outline stitch
    butterfly antennae— black outline stitch
    antennae tips— black French knots

6. This section is now ready to add to the entire quilt or to finish as an individual project.
7. For individual project:
    a. Add borders as desired.
    b. Layer quilt top, batting, and backing; quilt.
    c. Bind edges with straight strips of fabric, as shown on page 88.

Traditional Blocks

Make 2
Dk. pink/Butterfly

Make 1
Lt. green, dk. pink, yellow & purple/Egg & grass

Make 1
Blue, yellow & purple/ Egg & sky

Courthouse Steps Blocks

Make 9
Blue/Sky

Make 2
Lt. green/Grass

Make 3
Yellow, orange & dk. pink/Egg

Make 3
Dk. pink, yellow, purple & orange/Egg

Make 1
Yellow, purple & dk. pink/Egg

Make 1
Blue, yellow, dk. pink & purple/Egg

Special Blocks
*Note the piecing order on both blocks.

 Reverse
pieces 8 & 9

Make 1
Yellow, lt. green, dk. pink & purple/Egg & grass

Note pieces 6, 7, 8 & 9

Make 1
Yellow, blue & purple/ Egg & sky

MOUSE

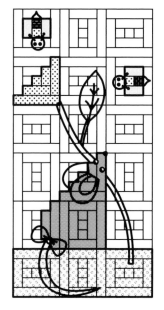

Color Photo: page 36

Size: 8″ x 15½″
18 Blocks (9-piece blocks)

Finished Block Size: 2½″ x 2½″

Materials: 44″-wide fabric
¼ yd. assorted blues for sky
Scraps of assorted light greens for grass*
Scraps of assorted medium browns for mouse*
Scraps of the following:
    Gold for flower and bee
    Pink for bow and ear
    Beige for bees' wings
You must be able to cut 1″-wide strips from these scraps.

Notions: green bias tape for flower stem; brown, black, pink, gold, and white embroidery floss

Directions

1. Color in the quilt plan and blocks with colored pencils to help eliminate mistakes.
2. Using either the speed-piecing method or templates, make the blocks shown above right.
3. When all the blocks are completed, sew the blocks together in horizontal rows as shown in the quilt plan above. Then sew the rows together, making sure to match the seams between each block.
4. Using the templates, T-2 Mouse on the pullout pattern insert, and the freezer-paper method, page 18, complete appliqué:

    pink bow to tail
    pink mouse ear to brown mouse ear
    ears to body

Traditional Blocks

Make 1
Gold & blue/Flower

Make 1
Med. brown & blue/
Mouse head

Courthouse Steps Blocks

Make 9
Blue/Sky

Make 3
Lt. green /Grass

Make 1
Med. brown/Mouse

Make 1
Blue & med. brown/
Sky & mouse

Special Block
See bee template on
pullout pattern insert, T-2 Mouse.

Make 2
Blue, gold & beige/Bee

yellow bees' heads to bees' bodies
green leaf to blocks
green bias tape stem to blocks

5. Complete embroidery:

    bow and veins in leaf—brown outline stitch
    eyes—black satin stitch
    "gleam" in eyes—white satin stitch
    nose—pink satin stitch
    bees' stripes and antennae—black outline stitch
    bees' eyes and antennae tips—black French knots
    bee's stingers—gold satin stitch

6. This section is now ready to add to the entire quilt or to finish as an individual project.
7. For individual project:
   a. Add borders as desired.
   b. Layer quilt top, batting, and backing; quilt.
   c. Bind edges with straight strips of fabric, as shown on page 88.

Color Key

Blues	☐
Lt. greens	▨
Gold	▨
Beige	☐
Med. browns	▨

BUTTERFLIES

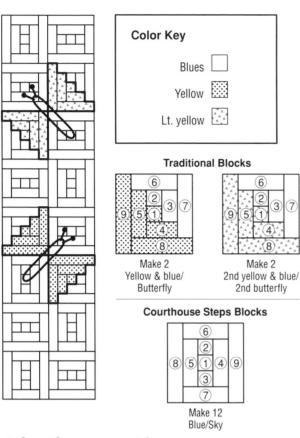

Color Key

Blues ☐

Yellow ▦

Lt. yellow ▨

Traditional Blocks

Make 2
Yellow & blue/
Butterfly

Make 2
2nd yellow & blue/
2nd butterfly

Courthouse Steps Blocks

Make 12
Blue/Sky

Color Photo: page 36

Size: 5½″ x 20½″
16 Blocks (9-piece blocks)

Finished Block Size: 2½″ x 2½″

Materials: 44″-wide fabric
¼ yd. assorted blues for sky
Scraps of the following:
    Light yellow for wings*
    Yellow for wings*
    Lavender for butterfly body
    Pink for butterfly body
You must be able to cut 1″-wide strips from these scraps.

Notions: black embroidery floss

Directions

1. Color in the quilt plan and blocks with colored pencils to help eliminate mistakes.
2. Using either the speed-piecing method or templates, make the blocks shown at left.
3. When all the blocks are completed, sew the blocks together in vertical rows as shown in the quilt plan at left. Then sew the rows together, making sure to match the seams between each block.
4. Using the template, T-6 Duck on the pullout pattern insert, appliqué the butterfly bodies to the butterfly wings.
5. Complete embroidery:

    antennae — black outline stitch
    antennae tips — black French knots

6. This section is now ready to add to the entire quilt or to finish as an individual project.
7. For individual project:
   a. Add borders as desired.
   b. Layer quilt top, batting, and backing; quilt.
   c. Bind edges with straight strips of fabric, as shown on page 88.

CHICKS

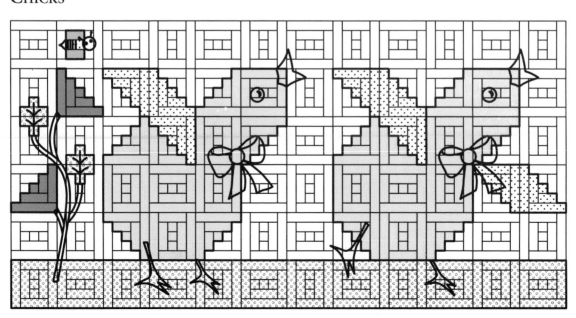

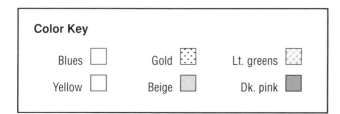

Color Key

Blues ☐ Gold ⌗ Lt. greens ⌗

Yellow ☐ Beige ▨ Dk. pink ▨

Color Photo: page 36

Size: 30½″ x 15½″
72 blocks (9-piece blocks)

Finished Block Size: 2½″ x 2½″

Traditional Blocks

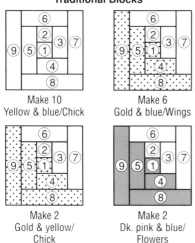

Make 10
Yellow & blue/Chick

Make 6
Gold & blue/Wings

Make 2
Gold & yellow/
Chick

Make 2
Dk. pink & blue/
Flowers

Courthouse Steps Blocks

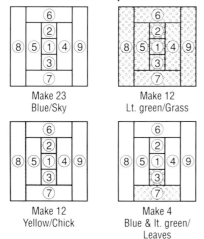

Make 23
Blue/Sky

Make 12
Lt. green/Grass

Make 12
Yellow/Chick

Make 4
Blue & lt. green/
Leaves

Special Block

Make 1
Gold, beige & blue/Bee

Materials: 44″-wide fabric
½ yd. assorted blues for sky
¼ yd. yellow for chicks
¼ yd. assorted light greens for grass and
  leaves
3″ x 40″ strip of gold for chicks' wings and bee
Scraps of the following:
  Dark pink for flowers
  Black for eyes
  Orange for beak
  Aqua for bow
  Light pink for bow
  Beige for bee's wings

Notions: green bias tape for flower stems;
  black, brown, white, orange, and gold
  embroidery floss

Directions

1. Color in the quilt plan and blocks with colored pencils to help eliminate mistakes.
2. Using either the speed-piecing method or
   templates, make the blocks shown at left.
3. When all the blocks are completed, sew the
   blocks together in horizontal rows as shown
   in the quilt plan on page 34. Then sew the
   rows together, making sure to match the
   seams between each block.
4. Using the templates, T-1 Chicks on the pullout pattern insert, complete appliqué:

   black eyes to head
   pink and blue bows to neck
   yellow beaks to head
   yellow bee's head to top of bee's body
   green bias tape stems to flower blocks

5. Complete embroidery:

   "gleam" in chicks' eyes—white satin
     stitch
   lines in bows and leaves—brown
     outline stitch
   bee's stinger—gold satin stitch
   bee's stripes and antennae—black
     outline stitch
   bee's eyes and antennae tips—black
     French knots
   chick's feet—orange satin stitch or
     several rows of orange outline stitch

6. This section is now ready to add to the entire
   quilt or to finish as an individual project.
7. For individual project:
   a. Add borders as desired.
   b. Layer quilt top, batting, and backing; quilt.
   c. Bind edges with straight strips of fabric,
      as shown on page 88.

GALLERY

Easter Parade by Christal Carter, 1991, Valley Center, California, 72" x 85". This collage quilt is made up of eleven individual patterns to form a charming parade of animals. Machine pieced and hand appliquéd; machine quilted by Barbara Ford.

It is not spring at our home without bunnies and baskets, eggs, and chocolate!

In "Easter Parade," a group of exuberant animals marches across the quilt through colored eggs and flowers. The bunny, duck, or chicks could be made into baby quilts by adding one or more borders. To personalize the bunny quilt, add a banner to his baton with an embroidered child's name or birth date. The basket could be changed to be fruit- or flower-filled, and the little mouse holding a flower might be used for the back of a child's vest.

Spring Sing by Christal Carter, 1991, Valley Center, California, 35" x 30". Log Cabin birds and a nest of eggs sit in a cherry tree. Leaves are appliquéd. Machine pieced and quilted by Carol Hayes of El Cajon, California.

It is such a joy to watch birds building their nests each spring. I love the thimble-sized hummingbird nests, low in the branches of the orange trees, with the tiny, dartlike birds whizzing in and out of the fragrant blossoms. There is always a hawk's nest swaying high in the tallest sycamore; it is as large and messy as the hummingbird's is compact and tidy.

"Spring Sing" pictures a pair of bluebirds nestled in a cherry tree with their future family. Carol Hayes made this quilt, using a wonderful blue "feathery" fabric for the birds and pale blue fabrics for the sky. The color of the birds could be changed easily to make them robins with red breasts or bright yellow canaries. You might even appliqué topknots and make red cardinals or bluejays instead.

Heart Strings, designed by Christal Carter, 1991, Valley Center, California, 44" x 42". This quilt was designed as a friendship quilt with the "heart strings" that connect friends in love. Machine pieced by Shirley Baker of Escondido, California; machine quilted by Christal Carter.

This charming quilt was made by my good friend Shirley Baker. Shirley had never made a quilt when she generously offered to give it a try. I thought it would be great to see how a novice quiltmaker, unfamiliar with rotary cutting, might handle this pattern. Here you see the delightful results!

"Heart Strings" was designed as a friendship quilt with a heart section for each friend to sign. It would also make a nice group quilt to give as a wedding or baby-shower gift. The hearts are then "tied together in love" with the ribbon bows that connect them. Vary the color scheme for a different look or add more hearts to make a larger quilt.

Amish Roses, designed by Christal Carter and stitched by Carol O'Brien, 1992, San Diego, California, 32" x 32". "Rounded Log Cabin" blocks form the roses in this quilt. Machine pieced and quilted.

One of my greatest summertime joys is nurturing the tree roses, so it seemed a seasonal book would not be complete without a rose pattern. Carol O'Brien gave my original design a wonderfully unique look by using Amish colors on a black background. A more traditional, romantic look could be achieved by using pink or yellow roses on a cream background.

Pastel Cherry Baskets, designed by Christal Carter and stitched by Linda Packer, 1992, San Diego, California, 45" x 45". This version uses reproduction fabrics to get a wonderful 1930s look. Machine pieced and hand quilted.

During my childhood, I spent many summer days high in the cool leaves of my Grandma's cherry tree in Medicine Lodge, Kansas. How I loved filling baskets with the shiny red treasures! Those memories prompted me to design the Cherry Basket Quilt. Linda Packer made two wonderful versions of the design, a "thirties" style in pastel-colored reproduction fabrics and the lovely brown cherry baskets with a stunning border print fabric.

Border Print Cherry Baskets, designed by Christal Carter and stitched by Linda Packer, 1992, San Diego, California, 33" x 38". Linda used a border print to achieve a rich feel to this machine-pieced and hand-quilted piece.

Tropical Fish, designed by Christal Carter and stitched by Patty Barney, 1992, San Jose, California, 50" x 34".
Patty added an aquarium tank border to frame the exotic fabrics in these tropical fish. Machine pieced by Patty
Barney; machine quilted by Christal Carter.

Who can think of summertime without envisioning water and fish? This version of "Tropical Fish" was made by Patty Barney, who used a brown "wood grain" fabric to create a border resembling an aquarium. Made from simple Off-Center Log Cabin blocks, the fish could be adapted for an ocean theme quilt or a summer garment . . . I can imagine them "swimming" around the hem of a skirt!

Pumpkin Frost by Christal Carter, 1992, Valley Center, California, 68" x 83". This collage quilt consists of seven smaller patterns, each adaptable to other projects. Machine pieced and hand quilted.

In this collage quilt called "Pumpkin Frost," I have attempted to capture childhood memories of autumn.

Each of the quilt sections can be made as individual projects. For example, the leaf section at the top of the quilt would make a wonderful table runner for Thanksgiving, while the rooster section would make a delightful kitchen wall hanging. The scarecrow is a good size and design for a boy's crib quilt.

Autumn Roses by Christal Carter, 1989, Valley Center, California, 34" x 40". This trellis design was used as a classroom project and adapted for use in the Autumn section of this book. Machine pieced and hand quilted with Broderie Perse appliqué.

In the west, October is the month when rose bushes flaunt their colors in a final grand farewell before winter. While "Autumn Roses" was designed with this in mind, you might also consider making a spring trellis in white and cream with pink or yellow roses.

Patsy Ann in Autumn by Christal Carter, 1991, Valley Center, California, 29" x 39". This quilt uses the "Split-Log Cabin" block for the background and features a hand-appliquéd doll and tree branch. It is easily adaptable to any season. Machine pieced, hand appliquéd, and hand quilted.

When I was nine years old, my Aunt Marita gave me a few yards of black calico fabric. Since my mother did not sew, this was a rare and wonderful treat! I proceeded to make a whole wardrobe for my doll, Roberta. She was very coordinated in her calico—from bathing suit to coat! I no longer have my beloved Roberta, but because she gave me such joy, I decided to design a quilt using Patsy Ann. Patsy Ann is the charming childhood doll of my mother-in-law. I placed her in an autumn setting, heading off to school, perhaps, amid the falling leaves.

The background consists of Split-Log blocks, with a large-scale autumn print for the border and leaves and a bird appliquéd in the "Broderie Perse" method (pages 19–20). She would be wonderful in any season—add a spring border of tulips or a winter border of holly and poinsettias.

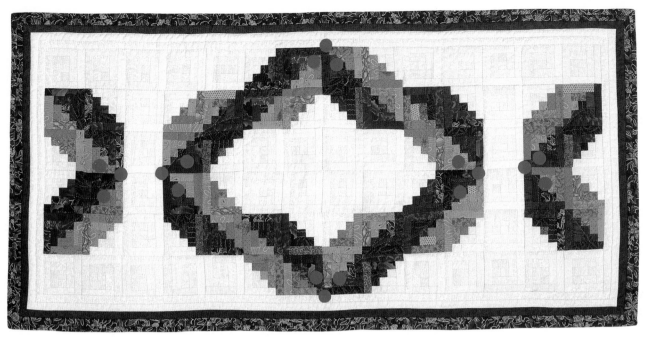

Holly Table Runner by Sandra Anderson, 1992, El Cajon, California, 20" x 40". Machine pieced and hand quilted.

How I love to go tramping about near our creek on a damp, cold morning, searching for the reddest holly berry bush. I tuck the holly among my winter arrangements and wreaths, beside the pine cones and acorns.

This table runner was made by Sandy Andersen, who added to my original design by forming a wreath of holly in the center of the runner.

Cabins in Winter, designed by Christal Carter and stitched by Elizabeth Haynes, 1992, San Diego, California, 47" x 40". Four cabins in a snowy mountain village could be expanded into a full-sized quilt or made as a one-cabin-unit wall hanging. Machine pieced and quilted.

There is nothing quite so cozy in winter as our little cabin in the mountains near Big Bear, California. The beds are piled high with quilts, and there are plenty of oak logs for the Franklin stove. Elizabeth Haynes made this charming version of the design, complete with smoking chimneys and glowing windows.

Poinsettia by Christal Carter, 1992, Valley Center, California, 40" diameter. This was machine pieced and quilted for use as a table topper but would work well as a wall quilt or as a repeat design for a large Christmas quilt.

While the California holly is not spectacular, the poinsettias found here are! They grow as high as the house and as big as dinner plates in brilliant reds, pinks, and creams. The largest commercial growers in the world are located along the coast near my home, so I use them extensively in holiday decorating.

This poinsettia was designed as a table topper for a round table, but it looks beautiful on the dining table or on a wall as well. It could also be a full- or king-sized quilt by repeating the poinsettia design six or nine times. A poinsettia print makes a beautiful border.

SPRING SING

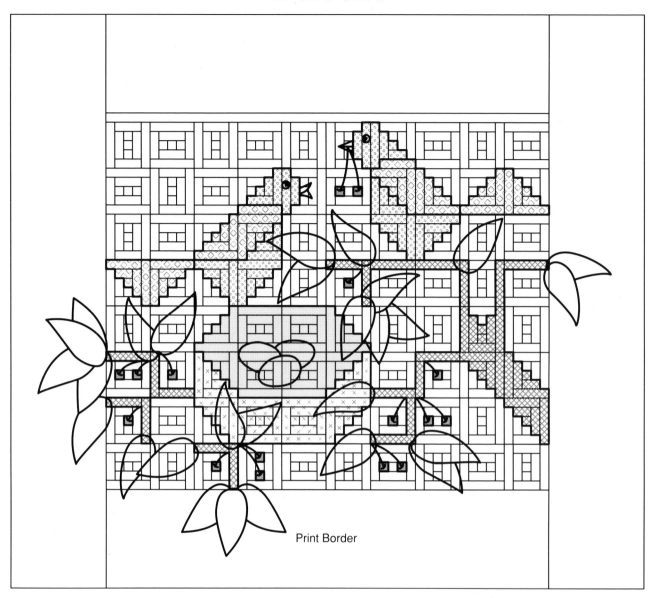

Print Border

Color Key

Lt. blues ☐	Beiges ▨	Red ▨
Med. blue ▨	Tans ☐	
Dk. blue ▨	Dk. brown ▨	

Color Photo: page 37

Size: 34½″ x 29½″
80 Blocks (9-piece blocks)

Finished Block Size: 2½″ x 2½″

Traditional Blocks

Make 8
Med. blue &
lt. blue/Bird

Make 6
Dk. brown, lt. blue
& red/Branch

Make 3
Dk. brown &
lt. blue/Tree

Make 2
Beige & tan/Nest

Make 2
Beige & lt. blue/Nest

Make 2
Tan & lt. blue/Nest

Traditional Blocks continued

Make 2
Dk. blue & lt. blue/
Bird

Make 2
Dk. blue & med. blue/
Bird

Make 1
Dk. blue, med. blue
& lt. blue/Bird

Make 1
Med. blue, dk. blue
& lt. blue/Bird

Courthouse Steps Blocks

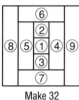
Make 32
Lt. blue/Sky

Make 4
Tan/Nest

Make 4
Lt. blue &
dk. brown/Branch

Make 4
Lt. blue & red/
Cherries

Make 2
Beige/Nest

Make 2
Med. blue & lt. blue/
Bird's head

Make 1
Dk. brown, lt. blue
& red/Cherries

Make 1
Dk. brown & lt. blue/
Tree trunk

Make 1
Dk. brown & lt. blue/
Branches

Materials: 44″-wide fabric

2 yds. coordinating print for border, binding, and backing
1 yd. assorted light blues for sky and eggs
⅛ yd. assorted beiges for outer nest
⅛ yd. assorted tans for inner nest
⅛ yd. dark brown for tree branches
3″ x 40″ strip of medium blue for birds' bodies
3″ x 40″ strip of dark blue for birds' wings and tails

Scrap pieces of the following:
  Red for cherries
  Assorted greens for leaves
  Gold for beaks
  Black for eyes

Notions: brown and white embroidery floss

Directions

1. Color in the quilt plan and blocks with colored pencils to help eliminate mistakes.
2. Using either the speed-piecing method or templates, make the blocks shown on page 48 and at left.
3. When all the blocks are completed, sew the blocks together in horizontal rows as shown in the quilt plan on page 48. Then sew the rows together, making sure to match the seams between each block.
4. When all rows are sewn together, sew an additional 1″-wide strip of light blue to the top edge. This will give some "airspace" between the bird and the border.
5. Cut 4 border strips, each 5″ wide. Add borders, as shown in quilt plan. (See page 86.)
6. Using the templates, T-10 Spring Sing on the pullout pattern insert, complete appliqué:

   black eyes to head
   yellow beaks to head
   blue eggs to nest blocks
   leaves to blocks and sashing

Note: Use the freezer-paper method, page 18, for eyes and beak, and the basted method, page 18, for leaves. Make 25–30 leaves and position them so that they show up against both the pale sky (use darker greens) and the border (use lighter greens).

7. Complete embroidery:

   beaks—brown outline stitch
   cherry stems—brown outline stitch
   "gleam" in birds' eyes —white satin stitch

8. Mark the top for quilting with soft, irregular curves in the sky area.
9. Layer quilt top, batting, and backing. Quilt on marked lines and around the birds, wings, nest, branches, leaves, and cherries. Quilt the border, using the fabric print for inspiration. For example, quilt around any leaves or birds in the print.
10. Bind edges with 2½″-wide strips of printed fabric, using the double-fold binding method on page 88.

Heart Strings

Color Photo: page 38

Size: 43″ x 41″

64 Blocks (13-piece blocks)

Finished Block Size: 3½″ x 3½″

Materials: 44″-wide fabric

2 yds. beige print for background

½ yd. each of 5 rose and burgundy prints for hearts, borders, sashing, and binding

1½ yds. coordinating fabric for backing

Notions: 8–10 yds. of narrow satin ribbon in a coordinating color; embroidery floss to match ribbon

Directions

1. Using either the speed-piecing method or templates, make 2 Traditional blocks and 2 Courthouse Steps blocks for each heart. Make 16 hearts total. I suggest making 3 hearts each from 4 of the fabrics, and 4 hearts from

the fifth fabric. This totals 16 hearts, made up of 64 blocks.

For each heart, make:

Traditional Blocks

Make 2
Heart color & beige

Note: If you are making 3 hearts of 1 fabric, make 6 blocks. For 4 hearts of 1 fabric, make 8 blocks.

Courthouse Steps Blocks

Make 2
Heart color & beige

Note: If you are making 3 hearts of 1 fabric, make 6 blocks. For 4 hearts of 1 fabric, make 8 blocks.

2. When all the blocks are completed, sew 4 blocks together from the same fabric as shown. Make 16 hearts.

3. Cut 16 beige sashing strips, each 1″ x 7½″; sew to bottom of each Heart Block.

4. Cut 32 beige sashing strips, each 1″ x 8″; sew to sides of each Heart Block.

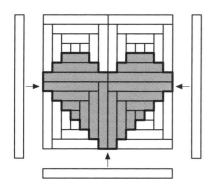

Assemble blocks into hearts.
Add bottom, then side strips.

5. For pieced sashing:
   Cut 12 beige strips, 1″ x 40″.
   Cut 6 rose strips, 1″ x 40″.
   Sew the strips together, beige/rose/beige, making 6 sashing-strip units.

6. Using 3 of the sashing-strip units, cut 12 pieces, each 8½″ in length.
   a. Sew the sashing strips and Heart blocks together into vertical rows of 4 hearts each.

   b. Cut 4 beige sashing strips, each 1″ x 8½″; sew 1 to the bottom of each vertical row of Heart blocks.

   c. Sew the 3 remaining pieced sashing-strip units between the 4 vertical rows of hearts.

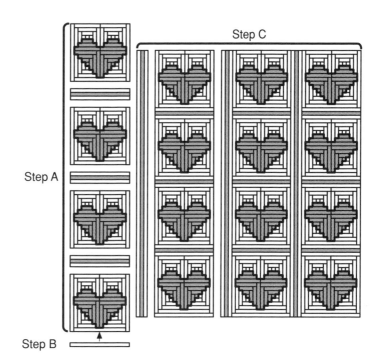

Step C
Step A
Step B

7. For borders, cut 4 strips, each 1½″ x 40″, from each of the 4 remaining rose and burgundy fabrics. Put 1 set of the strips aside for the binding. Sew the 3 remaining sets of strips together to make 4 border-strip units. I think it looks best to have the darkest fabric on the outside border and the lightest fabric on the inside. Sew the border-strip units to each side of the quilt top and miter the corners as shown on page 86.

8. Sew ribbon to quilt top, connecting the hearts. See quilt photo, page 38. Tie a bow above each heart as you go. Ribbon can be tacked in place with basting stitches. Add French knots all along the ribbon, removing basting as you go. If desired, embroider the names of friends and family on the hearts.

9. Mark top for quilting. Draw a heart in each Heart Block and cables in the sashing and borders.

10. Layer quilt top, batting, and backing; quilt.

11. Bind edges with 1½″-wide strips of remaining rose or burgundy fabric, as shown on page 88.

♠ *SUMMER* ♠

AMISH ROSES

Color Key

Black · Lavender · Dk. rose

Green · Med. rose · Lt. rose

Color Photo: page 39

Size: 32″ x 32″

81 Blocks (13-piece blocks)

Finished Block Size: 3½″ x 3½″

Materials: 44″-wide fabric

½ yd. lavender for border blocks
⅓ yd. each of 4 blacks for background
⅛ yd. each of 4 greens for leaves
1¼ yds. black for binding and quilt backing
Scrap pieces of 3 different prints in each of the following colors*:
  lavender, purple, pink, red, fuchsia, aqua, blue

You must be able to cut 1″-wide strips from these fabrics.

Note: Each rose requires 3 different fabrics.

Directions

1. Using the speed-piecing method or templates, make the following 13-piece Courthouse Steps blocks:

Courthouse Steps Blocks

Make 10
Black/Background

Make 21
Green & black/Leaves

2. Using the special Border Block Template, T-11 Amish Rose on the pullout pattern insert as a guide, make 28 border blocks.

Border Block

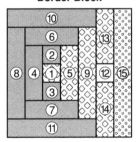

Make 28

To speed up the piecing of pieces #12, #13, and #14, cut 2 strips, each 2″ x 33″, of lavender and 1 strip, 1″ x 5″, of each rose color—purple, pink, red, fuchsia, aqua, and blue. Sew the strips together as shown in the diagram, with the lavender strips on the outside and the multicolored pieces in the center. Cut this unit into 28 sections, each 1″ wide.

Cut into 28 sections, each 1" wide.

Lavender					
Purple	Pink	Fuchsia	Aqua	Blue	Red
Lavender					

← 33" →

They can now be stitched to the border block as a unit. Add the final strip of green, #15, to complete each block.

3. Using the special Rose Block Template, T-11 Amish Rose on the pullout pattern insert as a guide, piece 22 Rose blocks.

Rose Block

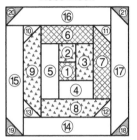

Make 22 assorted

Each Rose Block will contain 3 different fabrics of the same color and black triangles on the 4 outside corners. The blocks will look more like a real rose if piece #1 is the darkest fabric, pieces #2 and #3 are a medium fabric, pieces #4 and #5 are a light fabric, pieces #6 and #7 are a dark fabric and pieces #8 and #9 are the medium fabric. The matched "L" shape that is formed by adjoining fabrics looks like the curve of a rose petal. The last strips on the sides of the rose (pieces #14, #15, #16, and #17) should all be the same light fabric. This forms the circle of the rose. The effect is enhanced even more with the pieced corner triangles. Triangles #10, #11, #12, and #13 will be the same light fabric as pieces #14, #15, #16, and #17. Triangles #18, #19, #20, and #21 will all be black. See page 16 for a quick way to piece in the triangles.

4. After all 81 blocks are completed, assemble blocks in horizontal rows as shown in the quilt plan on page 52. Then sew rows together, making sure to match the seams between each block.

5. Mark top for quilting with diagonal lines through the background and leaf blocks and circles in the rose blocks.

6. Layer quilt top, batting, and backing; quilt.

7. Bind edges with 2″-wide strips of black, using the double-fold method shown on page 88.

CHERRY BASKET QUILTS

PASTEL CHERRY BASKETS

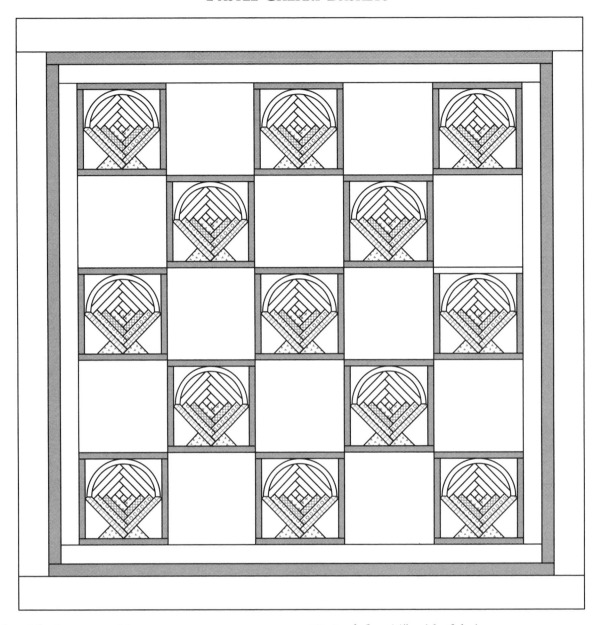

Color Photo: page 40

Size: 48″ x 48″
13 Traditional Log Cabin Blocks (17-piece blocks)

Finished Block Size: 7½″ x 7½″

Materials: 44″-wide fabric

Note: Use small prints if possible, but solids are fine if you have difficulty finding 5 similar prints. Fabric colors should be similar in intensity (darkness or lightness).

2 yds. white-on-white print for background and borders
½ yd. blue for borders
⅛ yd. total of 5 assorted fabrics in each of the following colors, for baskets and binding: lavenders, greens, yellows, pinks, peaches, blues, and rosy pinks

Scraps of reds for cherries
Scraps of greens for leaves
1½ yds. white-on-white print for quilt backing

Notions: small amounts of bias tape in colors to match baskets (approximately 8″ per basket); green embroidery floss for cherry stems

Directions

1. Using the template, T-12 Pastel Cherry Baskets on the pullout pattern insert, as a guide, make 13 Traditional Log Cabin blocks.

    Make 1 rose block and 2 blocks of each of the following colors; lavender, pink, peach, blue, green, yellow. Each block will contain all 5 of the fabrics in that color. Notice the piecing sequence indicated on the template and the fabric placement. The center of the block (piece #1) and piece C will be your first pink, pieces #4 and #5, your second pink, and so on. The Log Cabin Block itself should be a 5″ x 5″ square before adding the pieces from Templates A, B, and C. If your block is larger than 5″ x 5″, you will have to adjust Templates A, B, and C accordingly.

2. For each basket, cut 2 of Template A, 1 of Template B, and 1 of Template Br from the white-on-white print. Add ¼″-wide seam allowances to each template. Cut 2 of Template C for each basket in the appropriate color (same as the center, piece #1), again adding the ¼″-wide seam allowance.

3. Join B and C together, remembering to reverse the placement of B for one side of the basket. Sew the B/C units to the bottom side of each basket. Then sew A to each side of the basket top.

4. Cut 26 blue strips, each 1″ x 7″; sew the strips to each side of the 13 Basket blocks. Cut 26 blue strips, each 1″ x 7½″; sew to the top and bottom of the 13 baskets.

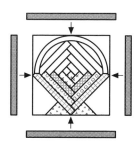

5. Basket handles may be cut from the template, T-14 Cherry Baskets on the pullout pattern insert, or from matching bias tape. Appliqué the handles as shown on T-12. Be sure to fold under the raw edges at each end of the handle.

6. Cut 12 squares, each 7½″ x 7½″, from the white-on-white fabric. Join white-on-white squares with Basket blocks, alternating the blocks in each row as shown in the quilt plan on page 54.

7. To assemble borders:
    a. From white fabric, cut 4 strips, each 2″ x 40″, for the inner border; sew to sides, then to top and bottom of quilt top.
    b. From blue fabric, cut 4 strips, each 1½″ x 40″, for the middle border; sew to sides, then to top and bottom of quilt.
    c. From white fabric, cut 5 strips, each 3″ x 40″, for the outer border (piecing as necessary); sew to sides, then to top and bottom of quilt top.

8. Using the templates, T-14 Cherry Baskets on the pullout pattern insert, and the freezer-paper method of appliqué, page 18, cut 35 red cherries and 35 green leaves. Appliqué cherries and leaves to each basket as shown in the photograph on page 42.

9. Embroider stems in outline stitch, using 2 strands of green embroidery floss.

10. Mark top for quilting in cross-hatch grid lines, 1″ apart, across the quilt surface. Do not mark cross-hatch lines on baskets, cherries, or leaves. Mark border with diagonal parallel lines, 1″ apart.

11. Layer quilt top, batting, and backing. Quilt on marked lines and around all baskets, cherries, and leaves.

12. To make binding:
    a. Cut the remaining basket fabrics into 1″-wide strips and sew them together in random order.
    b. Cut the resulting piecework on the diagonal into 1½″-wide strips.
    c. Sew these strips together to make a bias strip approximately 6 yards long.

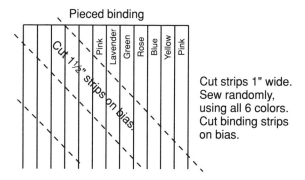

Pieced binding

Cut strips 1″ wide. Sew randomly, using all 6 colors. Cut binding strips on bias.

13. Trim square corners of quilt into softly rounded corners. Attach binding, using the regular binding method shown on page 88.

BORDER PRINT CHERRY BASKET QUILT

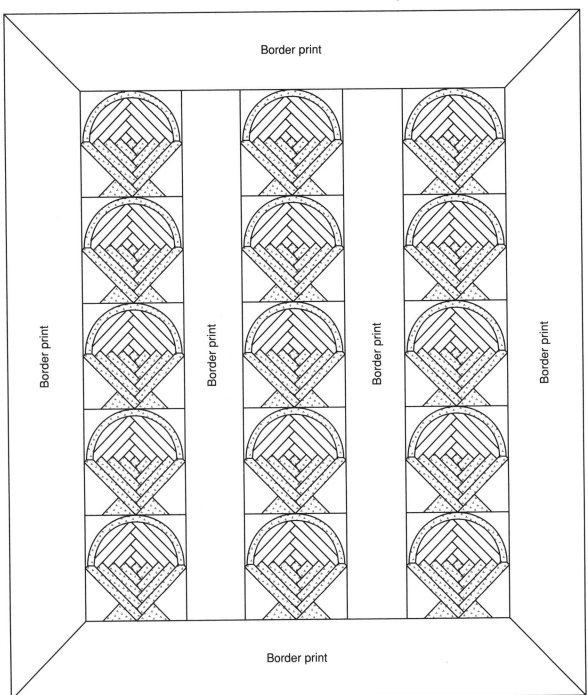

Color Photo: page 41

Size: Approximately 33″ x 38″
15 Traditional Log Cabin Blocks (17-piece blocks)

Finished Block Size: 6⅜″ x 6⅜″

Materials: 44″-wide fabric

1¼ yds. border print for sashing, border, and binding

Note: The border print must have 4 repeats of the same lengthwise stripe across the fabric width so you have enough for all 4 outer borders. If it does not, you need extra fabric.

⅔ yd. muslin or off-white for background
⅛ yd. each of 15 different browns for baskets
Scraps of reds for cherries
Scraps of greens for leaves
1¼ yds. coordinating fabric for quilt backing

Notions: green embroidery floss

Directions

1. Using the template, T-13 Border Print Cherry Basket on the pullout pattern insert, as a guide, make 15 Traditional blocks. Use 1 brown fabric for each basket. Reserve some of each brown for Template C (triangle pieces) and the basket handle. The Log Cabin Block should be a 5″ x 5″ square before adding the muslin pieces A, B, and C.

2. From muslin, cut 30 of Template A, 15 of Template B, and 15 of Template Br, adding ¼″-wide seam allowances.

3. Join B and C together, remembering to reverse the placement of B for one side of the basket. Sew the B/C units to the bottom side of each basket. Then sew A to each side of the basket top.

4. Using the templates, T-14 Cherry Baskets on the pullout pattern inserts, and the freezer-paper method of appliqué, page 18, cut 27 red cherries and 27 green leaves. Appliqué cherries and leaves to each basket as shown in the photo on page 41. Cut 1 basket handle from each brown basket fabric, using the template on T-14 Cherry Baskets, or cut a bias strip ¾″ wide and 8″ long. Appliqué handles as shown on the pullout pattern insert, T-13 Border Print Cherry Basket.

5. Sew Basket blocks together in 3 vertical rows of 5 baskets each.

6. Select a section of the border-print fabric for sashing, a section that you do not intend to use for the outer border. Cut 2 sashing strips and sew the sashing strips between each row of baskets as shown in the quilt plan on page 56. The width of these strips will be governed by the width of the design on the border print.

7. Cut 4 border strips for the quilt, making them long enough to miter corners (page 86). The width of these strips will be governed by the width of the stripe in the border print. A striped border print works beautifully and looks much more complex than it actually is.

8. Embroider cherry stems in outline stitch, using 2 strands of green embroidery floss.

9. Mark top for quilting. Mark muslin in cross-hatch grid lines ⅝″ apart. The quilting design for the sashing and borders will be determined by the print.

10. Layer quilt top, batting, and backing. Quilt on marked lines and around all baskets, cherries, and leaves.

11. Bind edges, using a section of the border print cut into 1½″-wide strips, as shown on page 88.

TROPICAL FISH

Color Key

Browns

Greens

Assorted fish colors

Color Photo: page 42

Size: 50″ x 34½″
80 Blocks (13-piece blocks)
Finished Block Size: 3½″ x 3½″

Materials: 44″-wide fabric
1 yd. brown for aquarium outer border and
    binding
½ yd. assorted browns for sand
¼ yd. each of 8 light to medium sea greens for
    water (or a good assortment of fabrics to
    total 2 yds.)
⅛ yd. black for inner border
Scraps of assorted colors for tropical fish:
    aqua, fuchsia, yellow, black, purple, and
    teal green
Scraps of dark sea greens for seaweed
1½ yds. coordinating fabric for quilt backing

Notions: green bias tape for seaweed stems

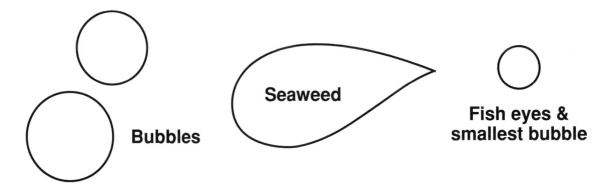

Bubbles

Seaweed

**Fish eyes &
smallest bubble**

Directions

1. Using the speed-piecing method or templates, make the following Traditional Log Cabin blocks:

Traditional Blocks

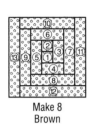 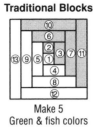 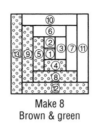

Make 8 — Brown   Make 5 — Green & fish colors   Make 8 — Brown & green

2. Using the Off-Center Block Template on page 10 (left) as a guide, make the following blocks: (Remember to make each fish block in a different color combination.)

Off-Center Blocks

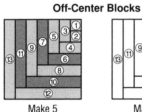

Make 5 — Fish colors   Make 54 — Green

3. When all 80 blocks are completed, assemble blocks in diagonal rows as shown below. Then sew rows together, making sure to match the seams between each block.

For a better effect, position the water blocks in such a way that the blocks with lighter colors are toward the top and those with darker colors are toward the bottom.

4. Cut off excess block parts ¼″ outside the diagonal center of each block as shown below. Run a row of stitching around the quilt, very close to the edge, to stabilize the bias edges. Be sure not to stretch as you sew.

5. For inner border, cut 5 strips, each 1″ wide, from black fabric (piecing as necessary for required length). Sew border to the sides, then to the top and bottom of the quilt top.

6. For outer border, cut 5 strips, each 6″ wide, from brown fabric (piecing as necessary for required length). Sew border to the sides, then to the top and bottom of the quilt top.

7. Using the freezer-paper method of appliqué, page 18, cut 18 assorted dark green leaves and 12 assorted green bubbles. Complete appliqué:

> *bias tape seaweed stems* to blocks
> *leaves and bubbles* to blocks
> *fish eyes (in colors that will make them visible)* to blocks

8. Mark top for quilting with horizontal waves in the water and on the sand—even marking over fish and seaweed. This will give the quilt an "underwater" appearance. Mark border as desired, depending on the fabric design.

9. Layer quilt top, batting, and backing. Quilt on marked lines and around each fish, bubble, leaf, and vine.

10. Bind edges with 2½″-wide strips of brown, using the double-fold method shown on page 88.

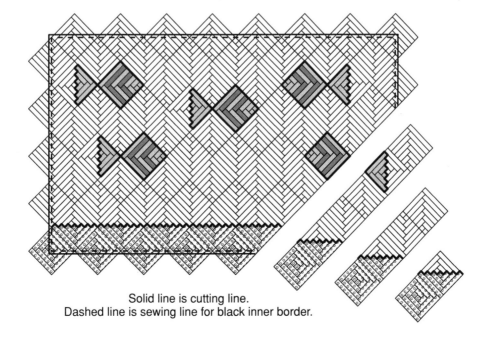

Solid line is cutting line.
Dashed line is sewing line for black inner border.

AUTUMN

PUMPKIN FROST

Color Photo: page 43

Finished Size: approximately 71½″ x 83½″

General directions for all of the Pumpkin Frost patterns:

1. Make a sample 9-piece block to check measurements and seam allowances. Sample block should be 3˝ x 3˝, unfinished, and 2½˝ x 2½˝, finished, after assembling the quilt.
2. Fabric requirements for individual projects do not include fabric for borders or backing. Fabric requirements and finishing instructions for the entire "Pumpkin Frost" quilt begin below.

Materials: 44˝-wide fabric

Yardage requirements below are for making all 7 sections of the "Pumpkin Frost" quilt. If you wish to make only an individual section of this quilt, refer to the yardage requirements given with the directions for that section.

4 yds. total assorted beiges for backgrounds
1½ yds. extra of one of the beiges for sashing
1¼ yds. total assorted dark browns for leaves, fence, acorns, stems, hat, and crow
1⅛ yds. total assorted reds for shirt, leaves, and rooster
1 yd. total assorted light browns for field, leaves, acorns, and pie crust
1 yd. total assorted oranges for leaves and pumpkins (Unlike other fabric color groups, you need more variety in oranges so you can have light and dark for the pumpkins.)
1 yd. total assorted golds for hay, leaves, and cider
⅝ yd. total assorted greens for leaves and cornstalks
⅝ yd. total assorted lavenders for leaves and pants
½ yd. extra of one of the reds for middle border
⅓ yd. assorted purples for leaves and tablecloth
¼ yd. extra of one of the golds for inner border
¼ yd. cream for face and cider label
1¼ yds. extra of one of the purples for outer border and binding
5 yds. of coordinating fabric for quilt backing

Directions for Finishing

1. Complete all 7 sections of the quilt. (See "General directions for all of the Pumpkin Frost patterns," above.)
2. Cut beige sashing strips 3˝ wide; crosscut into the following lengths. Measurements are based on a finished block of 2½˝ x 2½˝. Adjust measurements accordingly if your blocks are a different size.
   I, N - each 3˝ x 18˝
   J - 3˝ x 15½˝
   M - 3˝ x 43˝
   R - 3˝ x 23˝
   S - 30½˝
   T - 3˝ x 3˝
   U - 3˝ x 38˝
3. Using the quilt plan on page 60 as a guide, piece sashing in the following order. Do not stretch the sashing as you sew it to the pieced sections; otherwise it will not fit the next section of pieced blocks.
   a. Sew sashing "N" between haystack and three leaves.
   b. Sew sashings "S" and "T" to 2 leaf blocks as shown and attach to left side of haystack/leaves section.
   c. Sew sashing "U" to right side of haystack/three leaves section.
   d. Sew sashing "I" to bottom of two leaves section.
   e. Sew sashing "J" between rooster and two leaves section.
   f. Sew sashing "M" to top of rooster/two leaves section.
   g. Sew scarecrow to two leaves/rooster section along sashing "M."
   h. Sew sashing "R" to bottom of cider section.
   i. Sew haystack/three leaves section to cider section along "O."
   j. Sew scarecrow/rooster/two leaves section to haystack/three leaves/cider section along sashings "S" and "P."
   k. Sew top leaf section to bottom section along sashing "B."
4. For borders, cut:
   8 gold strips, each 1˝ x 40˝, for the inner border
   8 red strips, each 1½˝ x 40˝, for the middle border
   8 purple strips, each 2˝ x 40˝, for outer border

Note: If your fabric after preshrinking is less than 40˝ wide, you will need 1 more strip of each color for the borders.

5. Working with each set of border strips, piece 2 strips, each 74˝ long, for the top and bottom borders and 2 strips, each 85˝ long, for the side borders.
6. Sew the 3 colors, gold-red-purple, together to make 1 border unit for each side. Attach to quilt and miter corners as shown on page 86.

7. Using the acorn and leaf stem templates, T-15 Scarecrow on the pullout pattern insert, appliqué any remaining acorns and stems to quilt top.

8. Mark top for quilting:
   a. Mark swirls in all of the section backgrounds with the exception of the rooster section. Mark this section with radiating lines coming from the sun.
   b. Mark veins in all of the leaves.
   c. Mark sashing with a grid 1″ apart.

9. Layer quilt top, batting, and backing. Quilt on marked lines and around all objects. Quilt "in the ditch" around blocks in the scarecrow's shirt and pants.

10. Bind edges with 3″-wide strips of purple, using the double-fold method shown on page 88.

Two Leaves Section

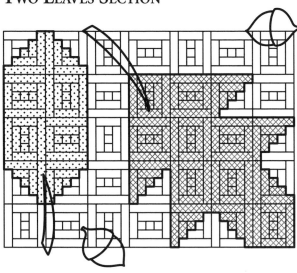

Color Key

Oranges ▨   Golds ⋰   Beige ▢

Traditional Blocks

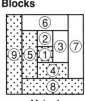

Make 6
Orange & beige/Leaf

Make 4
Gold & beige/Leaf

Courthouse Steps Blocks

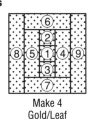

Make 13
Beige/Background

Make 8
Orange/Leaf

Make 4
Gold/Leaf

Color Photo: page 43

Size: 18″ x 13″

35 Blocks (9-piece blocks)

Finished Block Size: 2½″ x 2½″

Materials: 44″-wide fabric

⅓ yd. total assorted beiges for background
¼ yd. total assorted oranges for leaf
⅛ yd. total assorted golds for leaf
Scraps of dark and light brown for acorns and leaf stems

Directions

1. Color in the quilt plan and blocks with colored pencils to help eliminate mistakes.
2. Using the speed-piecing method or templates, make the blocks shown above.
3. When all the blocks are completed, sew blocks together in vertical rows as shown in the quilt plan above. Then sew rows together, making sure to match the seams between each block.
4. Using the templates, T-15 Scarecrow on the pullout pattern insert, appliqué the leaf stems. Appliqué the acorns after the borders have been added.
5. This section is now ready to sew into the entire quilt or to finish as an individual project.
6. For individual project:
   a. Add borders as desired.
   b. Appliqué acorns across borders.
   c. Mark top for quilting.
   d. Layer top, batting, and backing; quilt.
   e. Bind edges with straight strips of fabric, as shown on page 88.

THREE LEAVES SECTION

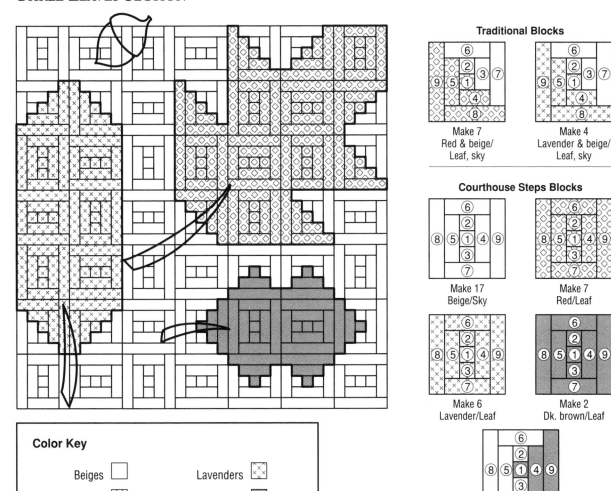

Traditional Blocks

Make 7
Red & beige/
Leaf, sky

Make 4
Lavender & beige/
Leaf, sky

Courthouse Steps Blocks

Make 17
Beige/Sky

Make 7
Red/Leaf

Make 6
Lavender/Leaf

Make 2
Dk. brown/Leaf

Make 6
Beige & dk. brown/Sky, leaf

Color Key

Beiges

Lavenders

Reds

Dk. browns

Color Photo: page 43

Size: 18″ x 18″

49 Blocks (9-piece blocks)

Finished Block Size: 2½″ x 2½″

Materials: 44″-wide fabric

½ yd. total assorted beiges for background
¼ yd. total assorted reds for leaf
⅛ yd. total assorted lavenders for leaf
⅛ yd. total assorted dark browns for leaf,
    stems, and acorn
Scrap of light brown for acorn

Directions

1. Color in the quilt plan and blocks with colored pencils to help eliminate mistakes.
2. Using either the speed-piecing method or templates, make the blocks shown above.

3. When all the blocks are completed, sew the blocks together in horizontal rows as shown in the quilt plan above. Then sew the rows together, making sure to match the seams between each block.
4. Using the templates, T-15 Scarecrow on the pullout pattern insert and the basted method of appliqué, page 18, add the stems to the leaves.
5. This section is now ready to sew into the entire quilt or to finish as a small project.
6. For individual project:
   a. Add borders as desired.
   b. Appliqué acorn across the border.
   c. Mark top for quilting.
   d. Layer quilt top, batting, and backing; quilt.
   e. Bind edges with straight strips of fabric, as shown on page 88.

LEAF TABLE RUNNER

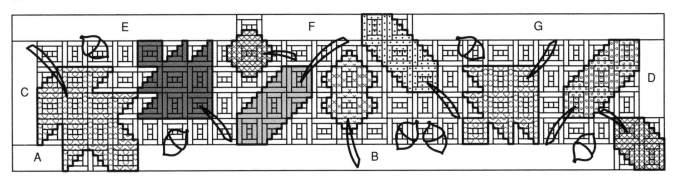

Color Key

Beiges	☐	Golds	⬜	Dk. browns	⬜
Reds	⬜	Lt. browns	⬜	Purples	⬛
Greens	⬜	Oranges	⬜		

Color Photo: page 43

Size: 65½″ x 15½″

105 Traditional Log Cabin Blocks (9-piece blocks)

Finished Block Size: 2½″ x 2½″

Traditional Blocks

Make 11
Red & beige/Leaf

Make 4
Orange & beige/Leaf

Make 4
Purple & beige/Leaf

Make 4
Gold & beige/Leaf

Make 4
Green & beige/Leaf

Make 2
Dk. brown & beige/
Leaf

Courthouse Steps Blocks

Make 35
Beige/Sky

Make 12
Red/Leaves

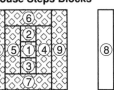

Make 6
Lt. brown & beige/Leaf

Make 5
Purple/Leaf

Make 4
Dk. brown & beige/
Leaf

Make 3
Orange/Leaf

Make 3
Dk. brown/Leaves

Make 3
Gold/Leaf

Make 3
Green/Leaf

Make 2
Lt. brown/Leaf

Materials: 44″-wide fabric

1⅓ yds. total assorted beiges for background (at least ½ yd. of 1 beige for the inner border)
⅓ yd. total assorted reds for leaves
⅛ yd. total assorted oranges for leaves
⅛ yd. total assorted golds for leaves
⅛ yd. total assorted light browns for leaves
⅛ yd. total assorted dark browns for leaves
⅛ yd. total assorted greens for leaves
⅛ yd. total assorted purples for leaves

Directions

1. Color in the quilt plan and blocks with colored pencils to help eliminate mistakes.
2. Before cutting strips for blocks, reserve ½ yard beige for inner border and enough dark brown to make 9 leaf stems.
3. Using either the speed-piecing method or templates, make the blocks on page 64.
4. When all blocks are completed, assemble blocks in horizontal rows as shown in the quilt plan on page 64. Omit the leaf blocks that will be used in the border. Then, sew the rows together, making sure to match the seams between each block.
5. Cut strips for border 3″ wide; crosscut strips into the following sections, piecing as necessary. Measurements are based on finished blocks of 2½″ x 2½″. If your blocks are a different size, adjust measurements accordingly.

    A - 3″ x 5½″
    B - 3″ x 48″
    C, F - each 3″ x 10½″
    D - 3″ x 8″
    E - 3″ x 23″
    G - 3″ x 25½″

6. Using the quilt plan on page 64 as a guide, piece sashing and remaining leaf blocks in the following order:
    a. Sew strip "C" to left side of table runner.
    b. Sew border strip "D" to dark brown/beige leaf block. Attach to right side of top, making sure to match the seams between the blocks.
    c. Sew border strip "A" and "B" to red, red/beige, dark brown, and dark brown/beige leaf blocks. Attach strip to bottom of table runner, making sure to match the seams between the blocks.
    d. Sew strips "E", "F," and "G" to dark brown/beige, gold/beige, and beige leaf blocks. Join to top of table runner, making sure to match the seams between the blocks.
7. Using the stem templates, T-15 Scarecrow on the pullout pattern insert, and the basted method of appliqué, page 18, appliqué dark brown stems to leaves.
8. This section is now ready to be included in the entire quilt or to finish as a table runner.
9. To finish as a runner:
    a. Add one or more borders to "frame" the leaves.
    b. Appliqué acorns across the borders.
    c. Mark top for quilting with an irregular swirling pattern to suggest leaves moving in the wind.
    d. Layer table runner top, batting, and backing; quilt.
    e. Bind edges, using 2½″-wide strips of fabric and the double-fold method shown on page 88.

Rooster

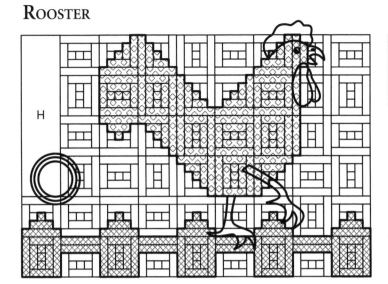

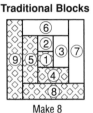

Materials: 44″-wide fabric

½ yd. total assorted beiges for background
¼ yd. total assorted reds for rooster
¼ yd. total assorted dark browns for fence
Scraps of orange and gold for sun,
 rooster's feet, and comb

Notions: black, gold, and white embroidery
 floss

Directions

1. Color in the quilt plan and blocks with colored pencils to help eliminate mistakes.
2. Using either the speed-piecing method or templates, make the blocks shown at right. Notice that 4 of the fence blocks have a special piecing sequence.
3. When all blocks are completed, sew the blocks together in vertical rows, omitting the 2 fence blocks in the left border. Then sew the rows together, making sure to match the seams between each block.
4. Add the left border. Cut 1 beige strip (H), 3" x 10½"; sew strip to remaining fence blocks as shown in the quilt plan. Attach pieced strip to the left side of rooster section, making sure to match the seams between the blocks.
5. Using the templates, T-18 Rooster on the pullout pattern insert, complete appliqué:

    orange waddle to rooster's neck
    gold feet to rooster's body
    yellow, orange, red sun in layers

6. Complete embroidery:

    beak—gold satin stitch, outlined in black outline stitch
    nostril in beak—black satin stitch
    eye—black satin stitch
    "gleam" in eye—white satin stitch

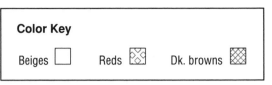

Color Key

Beiges ☐ Reds ▨ Dk. browns ▨

Color Photo: page 43

Size: 23″ x 15½″
50 Blocks (9-piece blocks)

Finished Block Size: 2½″ x 2½″

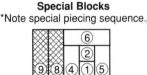

Traditional Blocks

Make 8
Red & beige/Rooster

Special Blocks
*Note special piecing sequence.

Make 4
Brown & beige/Fence

Courthouse Steps Blocks

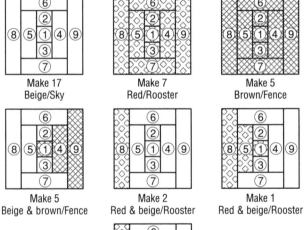

Make 17
Beige/Sky

Make 7
Red/Rooster

Make 5
Brown/Fence

Make 5
Beige & brown/Fence

Make 2
Red & beige/Rooster

Make 1
Red & beige/Rooster

Make 1
Red & beige/Rooster tail

7. This section is now ready to add to the entire quilt or to finish as an individual project.
8. For individual project:
    a. Add borders as desired.
    b. Appliqué orange comb to rooster's head, and into the border.
    c. Mark top for quilting with lines radiating from sun.
    d. Layer top, batting, and backing; quilt.
    e. Bind edges with straight strips of fabric, as shown on page 88.

SCARECROW

Crib quilt border strip

Color Key

Lavenders		Orange		Reds	
Lt. browns		Cream		Greens	
Dk. browns		Beiges		Golds	
Dk. orange					

Color Photo: page 43

Size: 45½″ x 45½″
294 Blocks (9-piece blocks)

Finished Block Size: 2½″ x 2½″

Note: This would make a wonderful crib quilt, but I suggest changing the colors of the falling leaves for better color balance.

Traditional Blocks

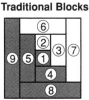

Make 13
Green & beige/
Cornstalks & sky

Make 11
Dk. brown & beige/
Hat & crow

Make 6
Orange & dk. orange/
Pumpkin

Make 5
Green and lt. brown/
Cornstalk, leaf

Make 5
Gold & beige
Straw

Make 5
Lavender & beige/
Pants & leaves

Make 3
Gold & lavender/
Straw & pants

Make 2
Lavender & gold/
Straw & pants

Make 2
Cream & beige/
Face

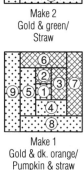

Make 2
Gold & green/
Straw

Make 2
Dk. orange & beige/
Pumpkin

Make 2
Red & beige/
Shirt

Make 1
Gold & dk. orange/
Pumpkin & straw

Make 1
Dk. orange & lt. brown/
Pumpkin

Make 1
Dk. brown, gold &
cream/Hat & face

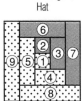

Make 1
Lavender & lt. brown/
Pants

Make 1
Dk. brown & gold/
Hat

Make 1
Dk. brown & cream/
Hat

Make 1
Gold & lt. brown/
Straw

Courthouse Steps Blocks

Make 78
Beige/Sky

Make 42
Lt. brown/Field

Make 25
Red/Shirt, patch

Make 22
Lavender/Pants, patch
& leaves

Make 15
Green/Cornstalk
leaves

Make 6
Dk. brown/
Hat, crow, patch

Make 4
Red & lavender/
Buttons

Make 4
Lavender & red/
Pants, patch

Make 3
Cream/Face

Make 3
Lt. brown & gold/
Straw

Make 2
Dk. orange/
Pumpkin & patch

Make 2
Gold/Straw

Make 2
Gold & beige/Straw

Make 2
Red & beige/Shirt

Make 2
Gold & beige/Straw

Make 1
Lt. orange/Pumpkin

Make 1
Beige & dk. brown/
Bird

Make 1
Beige & dk. brown/
Bird

Make 1
Red & dk. brown/
Shirt

Make 1
Lavender & gold/
Pants

Make 1
Gold & cream/
Face

Courthouse Steps Blocks continued

Make 1
Red & dk. brown/
Hat patch

Special Blocks
To make the following "corn" blocks, cut golds into
1" squares. Sew these into 3, 4, & 5 piece units
first, then add them to the block in sequence.

        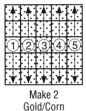

Make 1   Make 5   Make 2
Gold & beige/   Gold & green/Corn   Gold/Corn
Top of corn

*Note reverse piecing sequence.

Make 1   Make 1
Lavender, dk. orange   Lavender, dk. orange
& beige/Pants,   & orange/Pants,
pumpkin   pumpkin

Materials: 44″-wide fabric

2½ yds. total assorted beiges for background
and border
⅞ yd. total assorted light browns for field
½ yd. total assorted reds for shirt and patches
½ yd. total assorted lavenders for pants and
leaves
½ yd. total assorted golds for straw and corn
½ yd. total assorted greens for cornstalks
⅓ yd. assorted dark browns for hat, crow,
stems, and wooden poles
⅛ yd. orange for pumpkin
⅛ yd. dark orange for pumpkin
⅛ yd. cream for scarecrow's face

Notions: small black button for crow's eye;
green, gold, black, yellow, and brown
embroidery floss

Directions

1. Color in the quilt plan and blocks with colored pencils to help eliminate mistakes.

2. Using either the speed-piecing method or templates, make the blocks shown on page 68 and at left. Notice the special blocks.
3. When all blocks are completed, assemble in horizontal rows as shown in the quilt plan on page 67, but omit the leaf blocks in the border. Then, sew the horizontal rows together, making sure to match the seams between each block.
4. Using the templates, T-15 Scarecrow on the pullout pattern insert, complete appliqué:
   Use the freezer-paper method, page 18, to make the cheeks and eyes.
   Use the simpler basted method, page 18, for remaining appliqué. Extend the cornstalk template to about 26″ and appliqué it up through the corn leaves.
5. Complete embroidery:

   pumpkin leaf veins and tendril—black outline stitch
   mouth and eyelashes—brown outline stitch
   buttons—black French knots
   patches—straight stitch in various colors
   hay on scarecrow—irregular lines of brown outline stitch (See color photo on page 43.)
   crow's eye—small black button (may be added when quilting is completed)

6. Add left border.
   a. Cut 2 side strips, each 3″ x 18″, for sections L and K. Join strips to leaf blocks as shown in the quilt plan on page 67.
   b. Measure pieced side strip against quilt sides to make sure leaves on side strip line up with leaves on quilt; adjust, if necessary. Sew side strip to left side of quilt top.
7. This section is now ready to sew into the entire quilt or finish as a crib quilt.
8. For crib quilt:
   a. Add right border. Cut 1 square, 3″ x 3″ for section T. Cut 1 strip, 3″ x 38″, for crib border strip. Join remaining leaf blocks to T and border strip as shown in quilt plan on page 67.
   b. Sew pieced border strip to right side of quilt, making sure to match seams between blocks.
   c. Add additional borders as desired to finish quilt top.
   d. Mark top for quilting.
   e. Layer quilt top, batting, and backing; quilt.
   f. Bind edges with straight strips of fabric, as shown on page 88.

APPLE CIDER

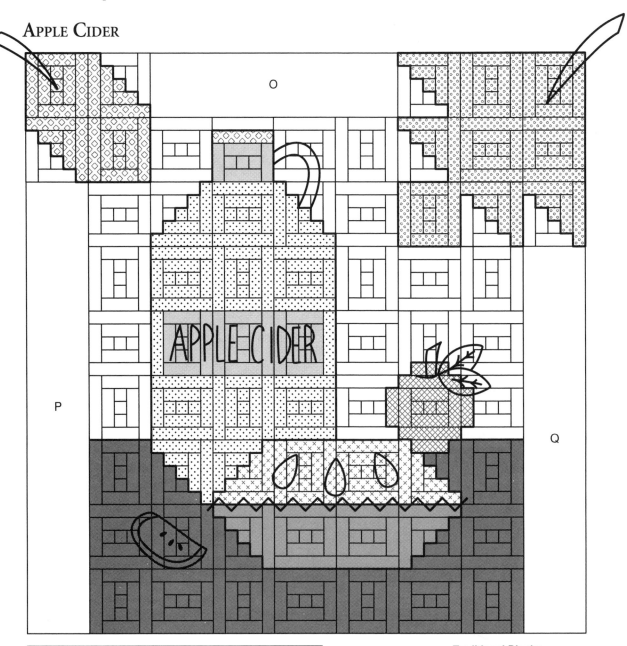

Color Key

Beiges ☐	Cream ▨	Dk. brown ◈
Red ▩	Oranges ⊡	Lt. brown ⊠
Golds ⋮	Purples ▦	Gray ▨

Color Photo: page 43

Size: 23″ x 23″ (including border leaf sections)
64 Blocks (9-piece blocks)

Finished Block Size: 2½″ x 2½″

Traditional Blocks

Make 4
Orange & beige/
Leaf

Make 2
Dk. brown & beige/
Leaf

Make 2
Gold & beige/
Cider

Make 2
Gray & purple/
Pie tin

Make 1
Lt. brown, purple &
red/Pie, apple

Make 1
Lt. brown & gold/
Pie, cider

Traditional Blocks continued

Make 1
Gold & purple/Cider

Courthouse Steps Blocks

Make 13
Beige/Sky

Make 12
Purple/Tablecloth

Make 7
Gold/Cider

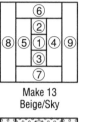

Make 5
Orange/Leaf

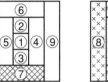

Make 3
Red & beige/
Apple, sky

Make 2
Lt. brown/Crust

Make 2
Dk brown/Leaf

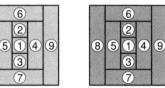

Make 2
Gold & cream/
Cider label

Make 2
Gray/Pie tin

Make 1
Red/Apple

Make 1
Cream/Label

Special Block
*Note special piecing sequence.

Make 1
Beige, dk. brown & cream/
Cider lid

Materials: 44″-wide fabric

⅓ yd. total assorted beiges for background
¼ yd. total assorted purples for tablecloth
¼ yd. total assorted golds for cider
⅛ yd. total assorted oranges for leaf
3″ x 40″ strip of gray for pie tin
3″ x 40″ strip of light brown for pie crust
3″ x 40″ strip of cream for cider bottle and label
Scraps of dark brown for leaf
Scrap of red for apple
Scraps of green for leaves

Notions: dark brown embroidery floss;
⅓ yd. large brown rickrack for fluting on pie crust

Directions

1. Color in the quilt plan and blocks with colored pencils to help eliminate mistakes.
2. Using either the speed-piecing method or templates, make the blocks shown at left.

Note: if you are making this section as a small project and not part of the whole quilt, you may want to eliminate the orange and brown leaves. If so, do not make the orange, orange/beige, dark brown, or dark brown/beige blocks. Instead, make 5 additional all-beige Courthouse Steps blocks.

3. When all blocks are completed, sew blocks together in horizontal rows as shown in the quilt plan on page 70. Then sew rows together, making sure to match the seams between each block. Do not include leaf blocks that fall in the borders.
4. Using the templates, T-17 Apple Cider on the pullout pattern insert, complete appliqué:

   white and red apple to tablecloth
   green leaves to apple
   brown stem to apple
   white jug handle to cider jug
   beige holes to crust
   rickrack along bottom of crust (See photo on page 43.)

5. Complete embroidery:

   apple seeds—dark brown satin stitch
   cider label—dark brown outline stitch
   leaf veins—dark brown outline stitch

   If you are making this section as an individual project, it is now ready to finish with your choice of borders. If you are making it as a section for the entire quilt, go to step 7.

6. For individual project:
   a. Add borders as desired.
   b. Mark top for quilting.
   c. Layer top, batting, and backing; quilt.
   d. Bind edges with straight strips of fabric, as shown on page 88.
7. Add remaining leaf blocks and border strips. Cut beige border strips 3″ wide; crosscut strips into the following lengths. Adjust measurements accordingly if your finished blocks are not 2½″ x 2½″.

   O - 3″ x 10½″
   P - 3″ x 18″
   Q - 3″ x 15½″

8. Using the quilt plan on page 70 as a guide, piece border strips to leaf blocks as follows:
   a. Sew brown/beige leaf block to side strip "P." Attach side strip to the side of the cider section, making sure to match the seams between the blocks.
   b. Sew orange block, orange/beige block, and side strip "Q" together. Attach to the other side of cider section, making sure to match the seams between blocks.
   c. Sew remaining leaf blocks to each end of border strip "O." Attach to top of quilt, making sure to match the seams between blocks.
9. This section is now ready to sew into the entire quilt.

HAYSTACK

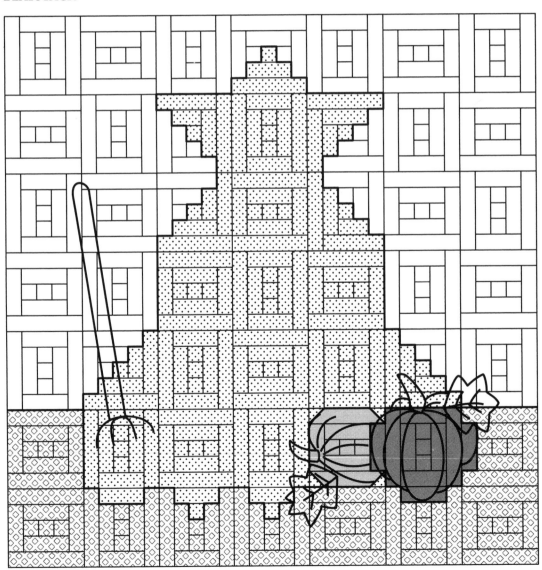

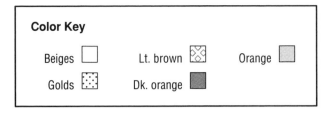

Color Key

Beiges ☐   Lt. brown ⊠   Orange ▨

Golds ⊡   Dk. orange ■

Traditional Blocks

Make 6
Gold & beige/Haystack

Courthouse Steps Blocks

Make 20
Beige/Sky

Make 11
Gold/Haystack

Make 4
Lt. brown/Field

Make 2
Lt. brown & dk. orange/
Large pumpkin

Make 2
Lt. brown & gold/
Haystack

Make 1
Dk. orange/
Large pumpkin

Make 1
Gold & beige/
Top of haystack

Make 1
Gold & lt. brown/
Haystack

Special Block

Make a regular Courthouse Steps block.
Cut off 4 corners and piece triangles in.
4 corners will be gold.

Make 1
Orange & dk. orange/
Small pumpkin

Color Photo: page 43

Size: 18″ x 18″
49 Blocks (9-piece blocks)

Finished Block Size: 2½″ x 2½″

Materials: 44″-wide fabric
½ yd. total assorted beiges for sky
⅓ yd. total assorted golds for haystack
¼ yd. total assorted light browns for field
Scraps of the following:
 Orange for pumpkin
 Dark orange for pumpkin
 Dark brown for pitchfork
 Assorted greens for leaves and stems

Notions: 1 yd. beige braided cord for rope
 around haystack;
 black and brown embroidery floss

Directions

1. Color in the quilt plan and blocks with colored pencils to help eliminate mistakes.
2. Using the speed-piecing method or templates, make the blocks shown at left. The small pumpkin is made of a special Rounded Log Cabin Block (pages 15–16).
3. When all blocks are completed, sew the blocks together in horizontal rows as shown in the quilt plan on page 72. Then sew the rows together, making sure to match the seams between each block.
4. Using the templates, T-16 Haystack on the pullout pattern insert, complete appliqué:

 green leaves and stems to pumpkins
 brown pitchfork handle to haystack

5. Complete embroidery:

 pitchfork tines—black outline stitch
 pumpkin tendrils—black outline stitch
 leaf veins—black outline stitch
 lines in haystack—brown outline stitch
 pumpkins—brown outline stitch

6. This section is now ready to sew into the entire quilt or to finish as a small project, such as a wall hanging or the back of a jacket.
7. For individual project:
 a. Add borders as desired.
 b. Mark top for quilting.
 c. Layer quilt top, batting, and backing; quilt.
 d. Bind edges with straight strips of fabric, as shown on page 88.
8. Add the braided cord to the top of the haystack when quilt or small project is completed.

AUTUMN ROSES

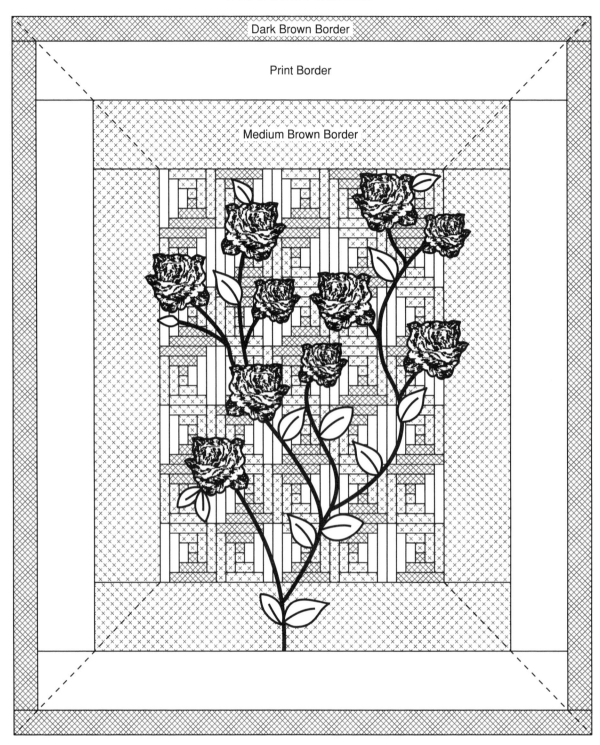

Dark Brown Border

Print Border

Medium Brown Border

Borders may be mitered or pieced "Log Cabin style."

Color Key

Blue ☐   Med. brown ⊠   Dk. brown ▨

Color Photo: page 44

Size: 31˝ x 37˝

35 Off-Center Traditional Log Cabin Blocks (11-piece blocks)

Finished Block Size: 3˝ x 3˝

Materials: 44″-wide fabric
1 yd. medium brown for trellis and border
½ yd. light blue for sky
½ yd. dark brown #1 for trellis
½ yd. floral print for border
½ yd. large rose print for appliquéd roses
¼ yd. dark brown #2 for outer border
¼ yd. red for binding
1 yd. for backing
Scraps of green for leaves if your floral
    print does not have enough

Notions: double-fold green bias tape for
    stems and branches

Directions

1. Color in the quilt plan and blocks with colored pencils to help eliminate mistakes.
2. Make 35 Off-Center Traditional Log Cabin blocks as shown below. These special blocks are 3½″ x 3½″ unfinished.

Off-Centered Traditional Log Cabin Block

3. When all the blocks are completed, assemble blocks in horizontal rows as shown in the quilt plan on page 74. Then sew the rows together, making sure to match the seams between each block.
4. For borders, cut:

   4 medium brown strips, each 4″ x 40″, for inner border
   4 floral strips, each 3½″ x 40″, for middle border
   4 dark brown strips, each 1¾″ x 40″, for outer border

   Attach each border with straight-cut corners as shown on page 74. (See page 86.)

Note: If using a large-scale or border print, cut border strips longer and miter corners as shown on pages 86—87.

5. Appliqué roses, using the "Broderie Perse" method on pages 19–20. Select roses from the ½ yard of rose print. Cut out roses, leaving a ¼″-wide seam allowance around each rose or leaf. Using green bias tape, appliqué vines as shown in the quilt plan on page 74. Be sure to hide ends of green bias tape under roses. Place roses on vines in a pleasing arrangement. Your roses may be a different size than the roses pictured, so you may want to alter the arrangement. Pin roses in place and appliqué to quilt top. Appliqué the leaves last. If your printed fabric does not have suitable leaves, use the leaf templates provided. Rose leaves often grow in three-leaf clusters, so be sure to include some of these to add to the realism. You could also add butterflies, birds, or small animals to the quilt top.
6. Mark the completed top for quilting. Mark the trellis with straight lines. Mark medium brown border in parallel lines, spaced 1″ apart. Mark the floral border with a single cable.
7. Layer quilt top, batting, and backing. Quilt on marked lines and around all roses, leaves, and vines.
8. Bind edges with 1½″-wide strips of red fabric, using the regular binding method on page 88.

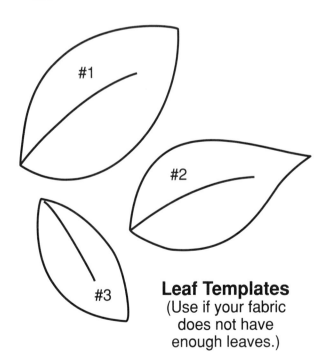

Leaf Templates
(Use if your fabric
does not have
enough leaves.)

Patsy Ann in Autumn

Color Key

Muslin ☐   Tan ▨   Beige ▨

Color Photo: page 45

Size: 33″ x 39″

20 Courthouse Steps Split-Log Blocks (9-piece blocks)

Finished Block Size: 5½″ x 5½″

Materials: 44″-wide fabric

1 yd. tan for background blocks and sashing

1 yd. large-scale autumn print for leaves and border

⅔ yd. muslin for background

⅓ yd. rust or other color to match border for pinafore

¼ yd. peach for skin on doll, dark enough to show up against muslin

⅛ yd. beige for center of blocks

⅛ yd. green or other color to match border for dress

⅛ yd. brown for tree branch

Scraps of the following:

    Dark brown for hair and shoes

    Light rust for stockings

    Dark rust for shadow in pinafore ruffle

1 yd. for backing

¼ yd. rust for binding

Notions: brown, green, black, white, peach, beige embroidery floss;
    3 very small buttons for dress;
    peach-colored fabric crayon or paint for cheeks

Optional: bird print fabric for bird to appliqué on branch

Directions

1. Color in the quilt plan and blocks with colored pencils to help eliminate mistakes.
2. Using the Split-Log Block template on page 10 as a guide, make 20 blocks. Begin the block by quick-piecing pieces #1, #2, and #3.
   a. Cut 1 strip, 2″ x 40″, of beige.
   b. Cut 2 strips, 1″ x 40″, of tan.
   c. Cut 2 strips, 1″ x 40″, of muslin.
   Sew the strips together as shown; crosscut the pieced unit into 20 pieces, each 2″ wide.

3. Cut 13 strips, each 1″ x 40″, from both the tan and muslin fabrics. Join 1 tan and 1 muslin strip together to form a double strip; make 13 double strips.
4. Using the double strips, finish Courthouse Steps Split-Log blocks as shown on page 10.
5. Cut 9 strips, each 1″ x 40″, from tan fabric. Using only 2 full strips and 12″ from a third strip, crosscut strips to yield 16 sashing strips, each 1″ x 6″. Sew sashing strips to blocks in vertical rows of 5 blocks each as shown.

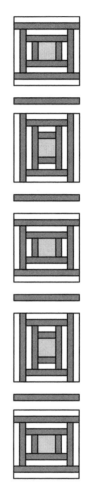

40″

| Muslin |
| Tan |
| Beige |
| Tan |
| Muslin |

2″

Cut each strip into 20 pieces.

6. Cut 3 sashing strips, each 29½″ long. Join sashing strips to rows of blocks.

7. Add the remaining sashing strips to each side of the quilt top, then to the top and bottom.
8. Cut 4 border strips, each 4½″ x 40″, from large-scale print. Sew to each side and miter corners as shown on pages 86–87.
9. Using template, T-19 Patsy Ann on the pullout pattern insert, and the basted method, page 18, appliqué tree branch to the quilt as shown.
10. Cut selected leaves from large-scale print, adding ¼″-wide seam allowance. Appliqué leaves on branch, using the "Broderie Perse" method (pages 19–20). Where leaves have been cut in half around border, appliqué the missing half onto the block section. If you

have a bird print, appliqué it to branch.
11. Using the doll templates, T-19 Patsy Ann on the pullout pattern insert, and the freezer-paper method of appliqué, page 18, appliqué doll to lower right corner of quilt. If peach fabric is too sheer and background shows through, you may want to line it with interfacing.

Note: Most of the embroidery may be done when the appliqué is complete, but the doll's face should be done beforehand. (See step 12.)

12. Trace the face and its embroidery lines onto an 8″ square of peach-colored fabric. Stretch fabric in an embroidery hoop and embroider colors as indicated on pullout pattern insert. For the best results, use 1 strand of floss on the face and embroider in the following sequence:

> *pupils*—black satin stitch
> *irises*—green radiating satin stitch
> *lashes, eyebrows, and nostrils*—brown outline stitch
> *"gleam" in doll's eyes*—white satin stitch on top of pupil and iris
> *upper and lower lips*—stitched separately in peach satin stitch

Note: Use fabric crayons or paints to "blush" doll's cheeks. If doll's legs and arms need more definition against the background, use 2 strands of brown floss to embroider an outline stitch around the edges.

13. Mark top for quilting with curved irregular swirls in background blocks to indicate leaves falling in a breeze. Mark some gathers in doll's skirt.
14. Layer quilt top, batting, and backing. Quilt on marked lines, as well as around branch, leaves, and doll. In border, quilt around leaves.
15. Sew 3 buttons on dress front. Do not sew through all 3 layers.
16. Bind edges with 1½″-wide strips of rust, using the regular binding method on page 88.

❄ *WINTER* ❄
CABINS IN WINTER

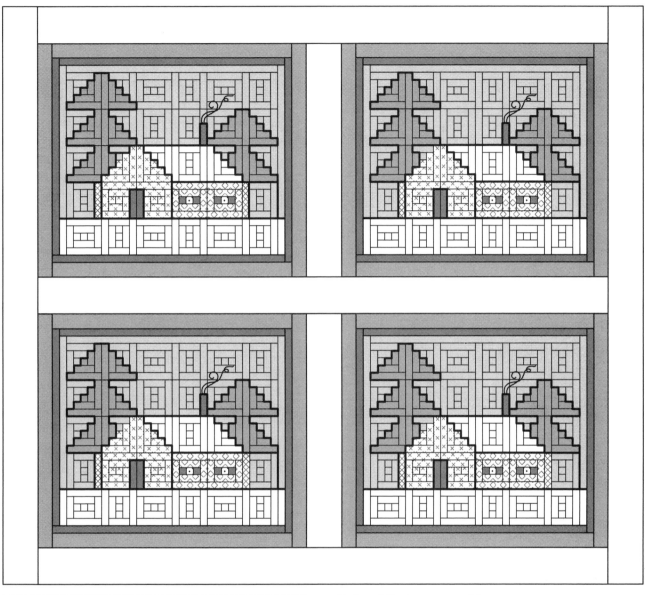

Color Key

Greens	Red	Med. brown
Blues	Yellow	Dk. brown
White	Lt. brown	

Color Photo: page 46

Size 46″ x 40″

120 Blocks (9-piece blocks)

Finished Block Size: 2½″ x 2½″

Traditional Blocks

Make 8
Green & blue/
Trees, sky

Make 1
White, blue & green/
Roof, sky, tree

Make 1
Lt. brown & white/
Cabin

Make 1
Lt. brown & red/
Cabin door

Courthouse Steps Blocks

Make 7
White/Snow

Make 5
Blue/Sky

Make 2
Med. brown, red & yellow/
Cabin windows

Make 2
Blue & dk. brown/
Sky & trunks

Special Blocks Traditional
*Note reverse piecing sequence.

Make 1
Lt. brown & red/
Cabin door

Make 1
Lt. brown, green & blue/
Roof, sky, tree

Special Block Courthouse Steps
*Note special piecing.

Make 1
Blue & red/Sky, chimney

Materials: 44″-wide fabric

2¼ yds. print for borders, backing, and binding
½ yd. dark green for borders
½ yd. white for snow
⅓ yd. red for borders, doors, and shutters
⅓ yd. total of assorted greens for trees
Scrap of yellow for windows
Scrap of dark brown for tree trunks
Scraps of red for chimney
You will need the following for *EACH* of the 4
   cabins:
   3″ x 40″ strip of light brown for cabin front
   3″ x 40″ strip of medium brown for cabin
      side
   ¼ yd. total assorted blues for sky (Each
      cabin's sky is a slightly different assort-
      ment of blues. Buy 1 yd. total of assorted
      blues if you want all 4 skies the same.)

Notions: 4 very small white buttons (door knobs);
   gray, green, and brown embroidery floss

Directions

1. Color in the quilt plan and blocks with colored pencils to help eliminate mistakes.
2. Using either the speed-piecing method or
   templates, make the blocks shown at left for
   each cabin section. Make 4 cabins, each time
   varying the sky and cabin colors.
3. When each group of cabin blocks is completed, sew the blocks together in horizontal
   rows as shown below.

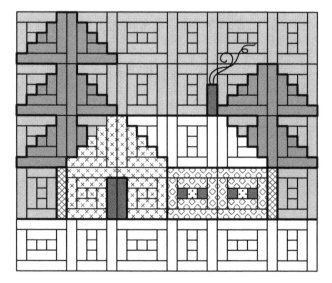

4. Sew the first 4 rows of blocks together (all except the row of snow blocks), matching the seams between each block. Then add the following pieces to give some "airspace" between the trees and the border.
   a. Cut 1 piece of sky fabric 1″ x 15½″ and sew to the top of the first row of blocks.
   b. Cut 2 pieces of sky fabric, each 1″ x 11″; sew 1 piece to each side of the 4 assembled rows of blocks.
   c. Cut 2 pieces of white fabric, each 1″ x 3″; sew 1 piece to each end of the row of white blocks.
5. Sew the row of snow blocks to the sky/cabin blocks.

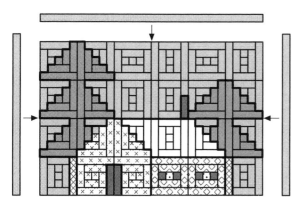

Add blue strips to top, then sides.

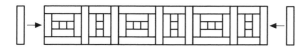

Row of snow blocks

6. When each cabin section is completed, add the following borders as shown in the quilt plan on page 79.
   a. Cut a 1″-wide strip of red and attach to the top and bottom, then to the sides of each cabin block.
   b. Cut a 1½″-wide strip of dark green and attach to the top and bottom, then to the sides of each cabin block.
7. Complete the quilt top by joining the 4 cabin blocks together with 3″-wide sashing and borders as shown in the quilt plan. Adjust measurements accordingly if your block sizes vary.
   a. Cut 2 sashing strips, each 3″ x 16″; sew each strip between 2 cabin blocks.
   b. Cut 3 strips, each 3″ x 41″, for sashing and top and bottom borders; sew strip between the 2 rows of cabin blocks, and sew borders to the top and bottom of the quilt.
   c. Cut 2 border strips, each 3″ x 40″; sew strips to each side of the top.
8. Using the embroidery instructions, T-20 Cabin on the pullout pattern insert, complete embroidery:

   chimney smoke—gray outline stitch
   vines—green outline stitch and lazy-daisy stitches.
   berries on bushes—brown French knots

9. The quilt shown in the photo (page 48) is quilted "in the ditch" between each block. If you want a more elaborate design, such as swirls in the sky, mark the top at this time.
10. Layer quilt top, batting, and backing; quilt.
11. Bind edges with 2½″-wide strips of fabric, using the double-fold method on page 88.

HOLLY TABLE RUNNER

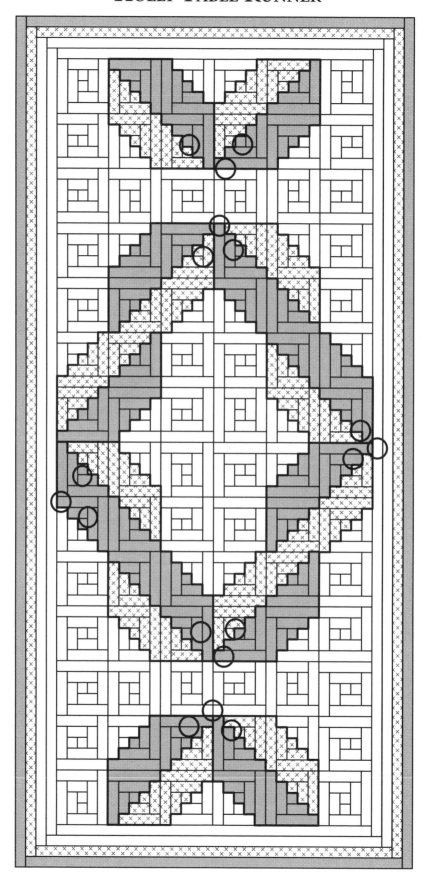

Color Photo: page 46

Size: 19½″ x 39½″

84 Traditional Log Cabin Blocks (9-piece blocks)

Finished Block Size: 2½″ x 2½″

Materials: 44″-wide fabric

1 yd. total of 4 white-on-whites for background
⅓ yd. total of 4 medium greens for holly
⅓ yd. total of 4 dark greens for holly
⅓ yd. holiday print for border and binding
Scraps of red for berries
⅔ yd. white-on-white for backing

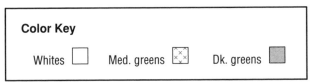

Color Key

Whites ☐   Med. greens ⊠   Dk. greens ▨

Directions

1. Color in the quilt plan and blocks with colored pencils to help eliminate mistakes.
2. Using either the speed-piecing method or templates, make the following blocks.

Traditional Blocks

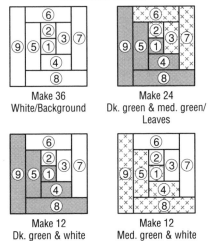

Make 36
White/Background

Make 24
Dk. green & med. green/
Leaves

Make 12
Dk. green & white

Make 12
Med. green & white

3. When all blocks are completed, sew the blocks together in horizontal rows as shown in the quilt plan on page 82. Then sew the rows together, making sure to match the seams between each block.
4. Cut 6 strips of white, each 1″ x 40″. Sew 1 strip of white to each end and each side of the runner. Then, sew a second strip of white to each end and each side of the runner. This gives some "air space" between the holly and the green border.
5. Cut 3 strips of dark green, each 1″ x 40″. Cut 1 strip in half and sew to each end; sew the other 2 strips to each side of the runner.
6. Cut 3 strips, each 1″ x 40″, from the print fabric for the last border. Sew strips to each end and then to each side of the table runner.
7. Using the freezer-paper method, page 18, appliqué red holly berries to the leaves.
8. Mark top for quilting with veins in the leaves.
9. Layer runner top, batting, and backing. Quilt on all marked lines and "in the ditch" between all blocks and along border seams.
10. Bind edges with 1½″-wide strips of print fabric, using the regular binding method on page 18.

Holly berry
Cut 18 (red)

POINSETTIA

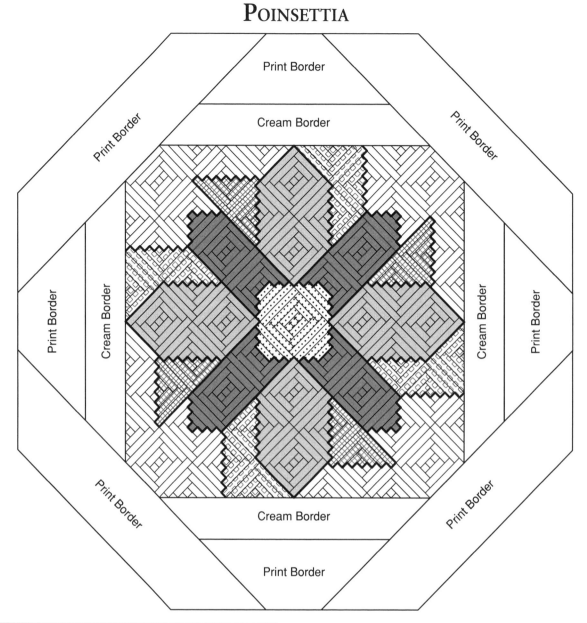

Color Key

Gold	Greens	Dk. greens
Reds	Cream	Burgundies

Color Photo: page 47

Size: approximately 40″ in diameter
57 Traditional Log Cabin Blocks (13-piece blocks)

Finished Block Size: 3½″ x 3½

Materials: 44″-wide fabric
2⅓ yds. cream for background, inner border, and backing
1⅓ yds. large print for borders and binding
⅓ yd. total of 3 reds for large petals
¼ yd. total of 3 burgundies for small petals
¼ yd. total of 3 greens for leaves
¼ yd. total of 3 dark greens for small leaves
⅛ yd. gold lamé for poinsettia center

Notions: ⅛ yd. fusible interfacing for backing the gold lamé

Directions

1. Color in the quilt plan and blocks with colored pencils to help eliminate mistakes.
2. Using the speed-piecing method or templates, make the following blocks. Back the lamé with fusible interfacing before cutting into strips. Be sure to test for iron temperature, since most lamés will not take high heat.

Traditional Blocks

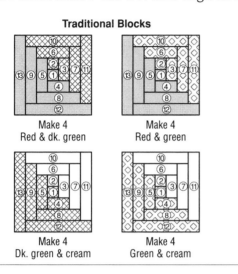

Make 4
Red & dk. green

Make 4
Red & green

Make 4
Dk. green & cream

Make 4
Green & cream

Courthouse Steps Blocks

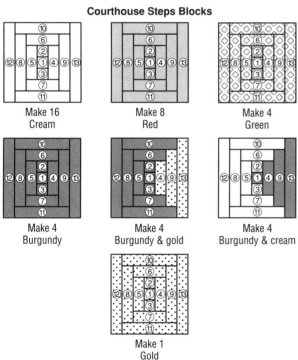

Make 16
Cream

Make 8
Red

Make 4
Green

Make 4
Burgundy

Make 4
Burgundy & gold

Make 4
Burgundy & cream

Make 1
Gold

3. When all the blocks are completed, sew the blocks together in rows as shown. Then sew the rows together, making sure to match seams between each block.
4. Cut off excess block parts as shown, ¼" outside the diagonal center of each block.

Run a row of stitching around the quilt, very close to the edge, to stabilize the bias edges. Be sure not to stretch as you sew.

Sew blocks together in 9 linear rows.
Then sew rows together.

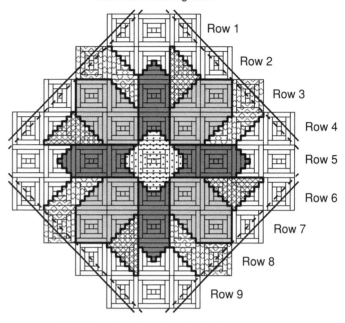

Row 1
Row 2
Row 3
Row 4
Row 5
Row 6
Row 7
Row 8
Row 9

Solid line is cutting line. Dashed line is sewing line for cream border strips.

5. Cut 4 strips, each 3" x 24", from the cream fabric. Sew the strips to the 4 longest sides of the quilt as shown in the quilt plan on page 84. Be sure not to stretch quilt edges as you sew or borders will be wavy. Press strips toward the outside of quilt. Trim the white strips even with the edge of the blocks on the short sides.
6. Cut 1 yard of the print fabric into 5"-wide strips for the outer border. Selecting sections of the strips that you especially like, sew 4 print borders onto the sides that have cream borders. Trim as before. Sew 4 print strips to the remaining 4 sides and trim.
7. Mark top for quilting with veins in the petals and leaves, and with circles in the center. Mark several rows of "echo" quilting around the flower.
8. Layer quilt top, batting, and backing. Quilt on marked lines and around the flowers in the border.
9. Bind edges with 1½"-wide strips of print fabric, using the regular binding method shown on page 88. The regular binding makes a slightly narrower edge finish, which is better for a table topper.

FINISHING TECHNIQUES

The projects in this book have been finished as quilts, but most can be adapted for other projects as well. The patterns could be used in garments, pillows, tote bags, or left unquilted and framed.

Be creative and try your own ideas!

Adding Borders

Borders may be added one strip at a time, or strips for borders may be sewn together and then mitered.

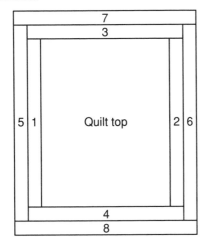

Add borders in numerical order.
It is like a giant Courthouse Steps Block.

Mitered Borders

1. Mark the center edges of the borders and design area by folding them in half and inserting a pin at the fold.
2. With right sides together, match borders to quilt top, following diagram. Pin in place at beginning and end of seam line. Be sure to match center pins.

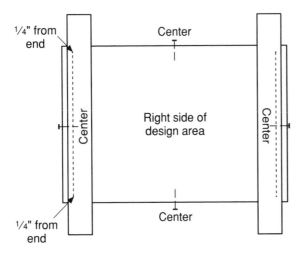

3. Stitch borders in place, beginning and ending seams ¼" from ends.
4. Press seams toward the borders.
5. Repeat with remaining two borders. (Seams will begin and end at the ends of the two previously stitched border seams.) Anchor these points with a pin.
6. Working on one corner at a time, fold top border under to form a mitered corner.

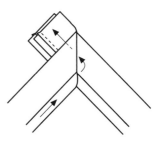

7. Align seam lines of border strips as indicated by arrows. Pin as shown. Press fold, remove pins, and press a firm crease at the fold.

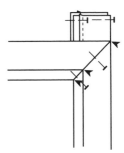

8. Leave pins in borders as shown.

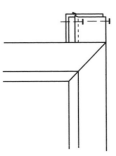

9. Fold borders with right sides together. Open seams and fold away from border. Insert pins through edges of border strips. Check underneath to see if pins are aligned with seams and adjust pins if necessary.

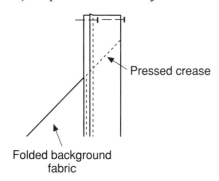

Pressed crease

Folded background fabric

10. Stitch on crease from design area to border edges. Trim excess ¼″ away from seam.

Preparing to Quilt

1. Cut backing and batting several inches larger than quilt top. Spread backing on flat, clean surface, wrong side up; anchor it with pins or masking tape.
2. Position batting on top of backing. Place quilt top on top of batting. Baste all three layers together from the center to the outside corners and edges. Baste outer edges.

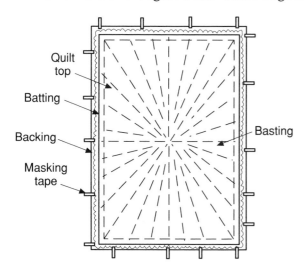

Quilt top

Batting

Backing

Masking tape

Basting

Hand Quilting

Suggestions for quilting designs are given with each pattern. I hand quilt most of my Log Cabin blocks, but they are difficult to hand quilt because of the many seams.

To quilt by hand, you will need:

quilting needles (I use the heavier size 10 needles to get through seams, and smaller needles in the border.)

2 thimbles (one for the middle finger of each hand)
2 rubber fingers (to go inside thimble and keep them from falling off)
quilting hoop (14″–18″ diameter)
small scissors
quilting thread

Use a single thread no longer than 18″. Make a small single knot at one end of the thread.

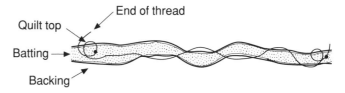

End of thread

Quilt top

Batting

Backing

Hand quilting stitch

The quilting stitch is a small running stitch that goes through all three layers of the quilt. To begin, insert the needle in the top layer about ¾″ from the point you want to start stitching. Pull the needle out at the starting point and gently tug at the knot until it pops through the fabric and is buried in the batting. Make a backstitch through all three layers at the beginning of the quilting line. Proceed to quilt small, even stitches on the marked line until the thread is 5″-6″ from the end. Then make a single knot close to the fabric. Make a backstitch to bury the knot in the batting. Run the thread off through the batting and out of the quilt top and snip it off. Repeat until the quilting is completed.

Important: Always begin quilting from the center of the quilt and work out. This will eliminate puckers. Make sure your backing is several inches larger than the quilt top to ensure there is enough fabric on the edges.

When you are instructed to quilt "in the ditch," this means to quilt along a seam so that the stitches are almost hidden in the seam line. Be sure to stitch on the side of the seam that has no seam allowances underneath.

Binding

There are numerous ways to finish the edges of a quilt. For the patterns in this book, I have used self-made binding strips. Strips are sewn, one at a time, to sides, top, and bottom of the quilt through all three layers (quilt top, batting, and backing). This can be done by hand or machine. Strips are then folded to the back and stitched in place by hand.

Regular Binding Method

1. Cut fabric strips the width stated in the individual projects. If strips are not long enough to fit the side of the quilt, piece the strips to the required length.
2. With right sides together, sew binding strips to the sides of the quilted project through all layers, using a ¼″-wide seam allowance.

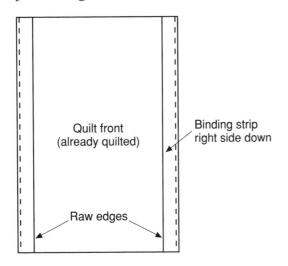

3. Open side bindings before sewing on top and bottom binding strips.
4. With right sides together, sew binding strips to top and bottom of quilt through all layers.

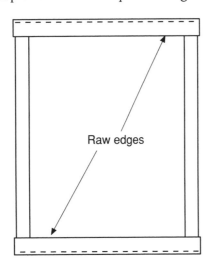

5. Bring the binding to the back of quilt. Fold raw edges under and blindstitch in place. Square corners or turn under corner for miter.

Fold raw edges under ¼".

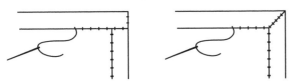

Square or miter corners.

Double-Fold Binding Method

This method requires twice the amount of fabric, because the binding is folded in half lengthwise before it is sewn to the quilt.

1. Cut the required binding strips, piecing as necessary.
2. Fold the strip in half lengthwise, wrong sides together, and press.
3. With right sides together, match raw edges of the binding and the quilt top; sew binding to the sides of the quilt through all layers with a ¼″-wide seam.

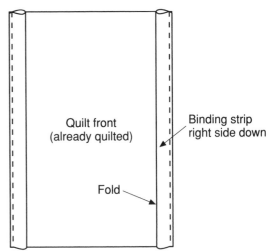

4. Open side bindings before sewing on top and bottom binding strips.
5. Sew binding to top and bottom of the quilt.

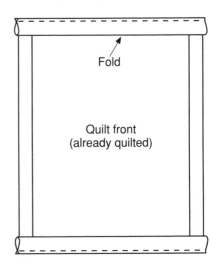

6. Bring the binding to the back and blindstitch in place. Square corners or turn under corner for miter.

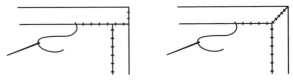

Square or miter corners.